Systematic Strategic Planning

A Comprehensive Framework for
Implementation, Control, and Evaluation

Systematic Strategic Planning

A Comprehensive Framework for Implementation, Control, and Evaluation

HAKAN BÜTÜNER

CRC Press
Taylor & Francis Group
Boca Raton London New York

CRC Press is an imprint of the
Taylor & Francis Group, an **informa** business
AN AUERBACH BOOK

CRC Press
Taylor & Francis Group
6000 Broken Sound Parkway NW, Suite 300
Boca Raton, FL 33487-2742

First issued in paperback 2019

© 2016 by Taylor & Francis Group, LLC
CRC Press is an imprint of Taylor & Francis Group, an Informa business

No claim to original U.S. Government works

ISBN-13: 978-1-4987-2481-4 (hbk)
ISBN-13: 978-0-367-37723-6 (pbk)

Library of Congress Cataloging-in-Publication Data

Butuner, Hakan.
   Systematic strategic planning : a comprehensive framework for implementation, control, and evaluation / Hakan Butuner.
      pages cm
   Includes bibliographical references and index.
   ISBN 978-1-4987-2481-4
   1. Strategic planning. I. Title.

HD30.28.B88 2016
658.4'012--dc23   2015021365

Visit the Taylor & Francis Web site at
http://www.taylorandfrancis.com

and the CRC Press Web site at
http://www.crcpress.com

To the memory of a great friend and a
wonderful human, Richard Muther.

Contents

PART II SYSTEMATIC STRATEGIC PLANNING (SSP)

PART III SYSTEMATIC STRATEGIC PLANNING SECTIONS

Preface

Basically, I felt the need for a systematic method of strategic planning. I wanted the method to be easy to understand and straightforward, based on fundamentals, and universally applicable to any type of business. Accordingly, I wrote this book with an aim to assemble the disconnected and disorderly ideas, processes, and techniques (written on strategy and business development) under one roof in order to develop a systematic methodology that is easily understandable and applicable.

Many books exhort managers to "think strategically" or prescribe "strategic leadership" to helicopter out of tactical day-to-day management, but few address how to make this happen. Where strategic analysis tools are explained, this is most frequently done conceptually rather than their actual application in strategic planning.

Moreover, as it could be a fond phrase to say that there is an "exact approach" or "systematic thinking" on this issue, my intention was to bring in a new perspective to the reader and, more significantly, to present the unique benefits the application of this methodology can provide.

This book presents a complete set of practical strategic planning techniques and tools. Where appropriate, I have refined these tools (from their original sources) to make them more user-friendly and effective. But, perhaps most important of all, you are guided in identifying in what circumstances you might use particular tools, and how, and in targeting them directly at achieving effective results.

Systematic strategic planning consists of a framework of phases through which each project passes, a pattern of procedures for straightforward planning, and the fundamentals involved in any strategic planning project.

This book aims at providing a detailed framework regarding systematic strategic planning. The book is organized into parts detailed as follows. The methods and techniques, case studies, and working forms presented will guide you through preparing a strategic plan for your existing or future business:

- Part I explains the steps to be taken before and after starting the strategic planning work.
- Part II provides the overall framework and characteristics of the simplified and full versions of systematic strategic planning.
- Part III describes the sections of systematic strategic planning in detail.
- Part IV provides a framework for implementation, control, and evaluation functions in a systematic manner.

This book is written chiefly for two groups:

1. Strategic planners—people who are skilled at making strategic plans, but who do not fully understand that a strategic plan for any business would involve variables specific to a particular business process. Their conventional approaches must be replaced with broader analyses, and individual and factual analyses of specifics must give way to group opinions and evaluation of convenience or preference.
2. Professionals—people not skilled in the techniques of strategic planning. This second group includes such people as owner-managers of small businesses, managers who are generally familiar with strategic planning, and department heads who are faced with a job that they plan to do themselves.

The content in this book has been prepared from the results obtained from applying the issue at hand to different application environments and their cause-and-effect relations. In order for the reader to obtain maximum benefit from the book, the issues on the sections are addressed as a whole.

This book is in fact an instructional manual. It has been designed to be specific, simple to understand, and easy to use. I hope you find it very helpful.

I owe a great debt of gratitude to all my fellow workers within my academic and business life, who contributed with opinions and efforts to the development of this book. Also, many thanks go to my dear brother, Okan, for his assistance and support during the typing of this book.

Most of all, I am very thankful to Richard Muther and his incredible innovation for planners. His is the best planning methodology I have ever seen or heard in my entire life, which is called *Planning by Design (PxD)*.

PxD simply lets you generate a methodology on any specific subject area. Many methodologies known and used by planners worldwide, such as systematic layout planning (SLP), systematic handling analysis (SHA), systematic planning of manufacturing cells (SPMC), multiple careers planning (MCP), etc., have been developed based on PxD.

I was very lucky to meet Muther and his lovely family and become his close friend. Thank you, dear great man. Also, special thanks go to my dear friend Lee Hales for his ideas on developing the systematic framework.

Dr. Hakan Bütüner

PART I
STRATEGIC
PLANNING
Before and After

Before beginning with strategic planning, businesses must have articulated their *missions* and *visions* and identified their basic *policies*. For this reason, proper formulation of mission, vision, and basic policies will play a determining role in the success of a strategic plan. Figure I.1 shows the before and after links of strategic planning.

Strategic plan outlines the path between the current status of business and the desired status to achieve. It helps the business to establish its objectives, goals, as well as the decisions to achieve these objectives and goals. It involves a long-term and prospective perspective. *This book is intended to explain how strategic planning can be done through a systematic method.*

Strategic plan provides guidance for the preparation of functional plans and business budget in such a manner that they reflect the objectives, goals, and grand strategies of the strategic plan during the implementation phase, as well as for basing resource allocation on priorities.

Functional plans help in the implementation of strategic plans by organizing and activating specific subunits of the business (marketing, financing, production, etc.) to pursue the business strategy in daily activities. Greatest responsibilities are in the implementation or execution of a strategic plan. Thus, functional plans directly address

Figure I.1   Strategic planning—before and after.

such issues as the efficiency and effectiveness of production and marketing systems, the quality and extent of customer service, and the success of particular products in increasing their market share.

Three basic characterisitcs differentiate functional plans and business strategies, which are as follows:

1. Time horizon covered
2. Specification level
3. Participation in the development

For functional plans, time horizon is usually short as for identifying and coordinatinge short-term actions undertaken in a year or less.

Short-time horizon is critical to implementing a business strategy for two reasons. First, it focuses functional managers attention on what needs to be done now to make the business strategy work. Second, the shorter time horizon allows functional managers to recognize current conditions and adjust to changing conditions in developing functional plans.

Functional plans are more specific than a business strategy to guide functional actions taken in key parts of the company to implement business strategy. Business strategy provides general direction. Functional plans give specific guidance to managers responsible for accomplishing annual objectives to ensure that managers know how to meet annual objectives.

Specific functional plans improve the willingness of operating managers to implement strategic decisions, when those decisions represent major changes in the current strategy of the firm.

Functional plans are delegated by the business-level managers to principal subordinates charged with running the operating areas of the business. Figure I.2 shows the relationship between functional and strategic plans. Similarly, operating managers establish annual objectives and operating plans that help accomplish business objectives and strategies.

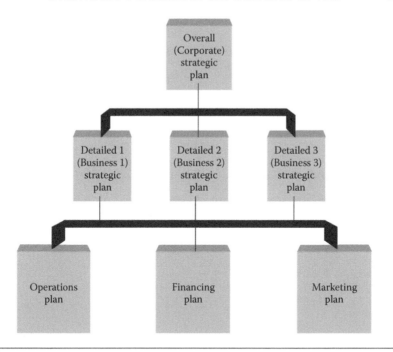

Figure I.2   Relationship between functional and strategic plans.

The involvement of operating managers contributes to successful implementation. Most critical, active involvement increases commitment to the strategies developed.

It is not possible to generalize about the development of plans across functional areas. Within each functional area, the importance of key variables varies across business situations.

1
Vision, Mission, and Basic Policies

Before beginning with strategic planning, businesses must have articulated their *missions* and *visions*, and identified their *basic policies*. Mission, vision, and basic policies are elements that form the corporate identity of a business. A business cannot be identified solely by its name, logo, or workflow. The know-how, experience, and expertise of the business and the corporate attitude it has developed create a specific corporate identity. One of the functions of strategic planning is to establish a stronger link between the corporate identity of the business and the products/services it offers.

While a significant portion of employees in a business have an idea about the identity of the unit in which they work, they hardly conceive a corporate identity that involves the whole business within the framework of mission, vision, and basic policies. Strategic planning guides individuals through understanding this integrity in a disciplined manner.

As a result of the formulation of mission, vision, and basic policies, the framework in which the business will reach the desired point and will come out through the establishment of strategic objectives and goals. For this reason, proper formulation of mission, vision, and basic policies will play a determining role for the success of a strategic plan.

1.1 Vision

Vision symbolizes the future of a business. It is a strong expression of what the business wants to achieve in the long term. Vision is a connective element among the different units of a business. Therefore, it plays a much more important role in businesses that fulfill a multitude of functions.

Vision is an ambitious albeit attainable expression of the future the business wants for itself. This expression of future must also encourage employees and decision-makers to move forward. Together with statement of mission, vision forms the roof of the strategic planning process of the business:

- It describes a future that is more different and better than today.
- It gives hope to people that it can be achieved.
- It is inspiring and encourages people to achieve the objective.
- It must be communicated to the people within the organization as a set of goals.
- It must be properly shaped.
- It must be refined.
- It must be achievable.
- It helps to define goals.
- It guides the generation of strategy.
- It must be short, consistent, focused, and flexible.

A strong vision should have the following characteristics:

- Idealist; it must be cordially developed and felt.
- Original; it has a clear affiliation with the business.
- Distinctive; it distinguishes the business from others.
- Attractive; it attracts the attention of people both within and outside the business.

In order to understand the vision of your business, you need to ask the following questions:

- Does your business have a vision? What is that vision?
- How do you communicate your vision to your clients/employees/vendors?
- How do you measure your progress toward your vision?

For developing a vision, the following important questions to be asked (Wickham 2004):

- What will be the source of the value to be created in the new world?
- Who will be involved in this new world? (i.e., Who are the stakeholders?)

- Why will those involved be better off than they are at present?
- In what way will they gain (financially, socially, etc.)?
- What new relationships will need to be developed?
- What is the nature of the relationships that will be built?

Examples of vision:

- *British Airways* (*1998*): "Become a leader in world transport."
- *Southwest Airlines*: "Open the sky to ordinary people."
- *Stanford University* (*1940*): "Be the Harvard of the West."
- *Sony* (*1950*): "Become the company most known for changing the worldwide poor-quality image of Japanese products."
- *General Electric* (*1980*): "Become the number one in every market we serve, having the strength of a big company combined with the leanness and agility of a small company."
- *PxD* (*Planning by Design*) *Institute*: "Become a leading institution in the effort of supporting planners to upgrade their professional competencies at international standards."

1.2 Mission

Mission is the reason for being of a business; it clearly states what the business does, how and for whom it works. Mission forms the basis of strategic planning. Mission statement of a business is an umbrella concept that involves all products/services and activities offered by the business (Wickham 2004):

- Codifies (i.e., gives form and communicates) vision
- Encourages analysis of the venture
- Defines the scope of the business (i.e., what to achieve and how to achieve)
- Provides a guide for setting objectives
- Clarifies strategic options (i.e., guidance on what paths might be taken)
- Communication tool
- Constant point of reference during periods of change
- It does not involve time dimension
- It is expressed in a brief, clear, and striking fashion

Points to consider while establishing a mission (Wickham 2004):

- Product/service scope
- Customer groups served
- Benefits offered and customer needs served
- Sources of sustainable competitive advantage
- What the business aims to achieve (i.e., financial performane, market leader, significant player, etc.)

Definition of mission:

Wickham (2004) stated that, as an example, the definition of mission could be, "The {*business*} aims to use its {*competitive advantage*} to achieve/maintain {*aspirations*} in providing {*product scope*} which offers {*benefits*} to satisfy the {*needs*} of {*customer scope*}. In doing this the business will at all times strive to uphold {*values*}."

- It must establish the direction of strategic planning by dwelling on the sanctions on groups with critical role in the performance of the business, such as clients, shareholders, employees, and vendors.
- It must identify how the business will differ in the future.
- It must include the values that create the corporate identity of the business and define the social rationale for its long-term existence.
- Uniformity of objectives must be ensured within the business, through the involvement of management.
- It must express how clients perceive the business.
- It must be in the form of a message to be conveyed within and/or outside the sector, reflecting the image, activities, and objective of the business.

Examples of mission:

- *Honda*: "We are dedicated to supplying products of the highest quality, yet at a reasonable price for worldwide customer satisfaction."
- *Walmart*: "Enable the middle class to buy the goods which upper class can buy."
- *Southwest*: "Dedication to the highest quality of customer service delivered with a sense of warmth, friendliness, individual pride, and company spirit."

1.3 Basic Policies

Basic policies are an expression of the basic values of a business. They express the values, management style, and codes of conduct of the business. Examples of basic policies may include transparency, equality, participation, moral values, and quality understanding.

Laying down the basic policies of a business is important for strategic planning since policies form the basis of the values and beliefs behind the vision and mission of a business. These policies provide guidance for the decisions, choices, and strategies of a business. Policies realized are strong instruments in changing business identity and motivating employees.

Policies may be written and formal or unwritten and informal. The positive reasons for informal, unwritten policies are usually associated with some strategic need for competitive secrecy. However, unwritten, informal policies may be contrary to the long-term success of a strategy.

A well-expressed statement of policies must be as follows:

- It must set out basic values and beliefs in a clear and precise manner.
- It must state the main idea relating to the conditions under which the employees will best perform their tasks.
- It must support the system and processes that would enable the business to achieve its vision.

What should the definition of basic policies include?

- What is the operational philosophy of the business?
- What are the values, standards, and ideals forming the basis of the operations of the business?
- What are the values and beliefs adopted by the employees of the business?

Statement of policies concerns the following three main areas:

1. *People*: Employees of the business and people outside the business.
2. *Processes*: Management, decision-making, and service production processes of the business.

3. *Performance*: Expectations regarding the quality of services and/or products produced by the business.

Examples of statement of policies are as follows:

- "Participation, transparency, and equality are essential in the decision-making process."
- "We do not compromise on quality in the services we offer to our clients."

2

STRATEGIC PLANNING

Strategic planning outlines the path between the current status of the business and the desired status to attain. It requires the business to identify its objectives, goals, and the decisions to enable achievement of these objectives and goals. It involves a long-term prospective perspective. Strategic plan provides guidance for the preparation of functional plans and business budget in such a manner that they reflect the objectives, goals, and grand strategies of the strategic plan during the implementation phase, as well as for accountability and basing resource allocation on priorities:

- It must be consistent with the mission and vision.
- It consists of steps required to be taken so that the business can achieve its goals.
- It needs to be reviewed constantly.
- It must provide guidance for the organizational structure.

In this framework, strategic planning can be defined as follows:

- It is the planning of results. It focuses on results, not inputs.
- It is the planning of change. It tries to ensure that change occurs in the desired direction and supports change. It is dynamic and orients the future. It needs to be reviewed regularly and be adapted to evolving conditions.
- It is realistic. It describes the desired and achievable future.
- It is an instrument of quality management. It evaluates and shapes up in a disciplined and systematic manner, how a business defines itself, what it does, and why it does these, and produces the basic decisions and actions guiding these processes.

- It forms the basis for accountability. It lays the foundations for monitoring, evaluating, and supervising how and to what extent the targeted results have been achieved.
- It is a participatory approach. It is imperative that strategic planning process be fully supported by the highest level executive of the organization. Furthermore, strategic planning cannot be successful without the contribution, joint effort and support of related parties, other officials, administrators, and staff members at any level.

On the other hand, strategic planning has the following properties:

- It is not intended to respond to day-to-day needs. It is a long-term approach.
- It is a flexible instrument that can be adapted to the different structures and needs of businesses.
- It is not solely a document. The preparation of strategic plan is not sufficient for its realization. Ownership and activation are needed. The strategic plan document itself is not only essential, but also the strategic planning process.
- While resources are taken into consideration in strategic planning process, annual budget and resource demands should not shape strategic plans, but the strategic plan must guide functional plans and budget.
- In summary, strategic planning helps a business answer the following four basic questions:
  - Where are we?
  - Where do we want to go?
  - How can we reach our target destination?
  - How can we monitor and evaluate our success?

Answers to these questions make up the strategic planning process. The answer to the question, *"Where are we?"* enables a status analysis involving a comprehensive review and evaluation of the internal and external environment in which the business operates.

The answer to the question, *"What do we want to achieve?"* lays down the strategic objectives that represent the conceptual results toward which efforts and actions will be designed, as well as the goals that represent measurable results required to be achieved so that the objectives can be attained, in light of the mission, which is a brief expression of the reason for being of the business; the vision, which is a conceptual, realistic, and brief expression of the desired future; and the basic principles that guide the operations of the business.

The main strategies, which are the decisions to be used to achieve strategic objectives and goals, answer the question, *"How can we reach our target destination?"*

Finally, the compilation of management information, monitoring for the reporting of implementation plan, the evaluation of the extent to which the results achieved are consistent with the previously established mission, vision, basic policies, objectives, and goals (i.e., performance evaluation) and the assessment process implying the review of the plan in light of the results answer the question, *"How can we monitor and evaluate our success?"* The considerations outlined previously will be described in more detail in the following chapters.

2.1 Strategy and Planning

Planning is designed based on a known future and it is related to results expected to be obtained in static environments. Strategy creation is a dynamic event. It is intended for the positioning of organization to achieve the planned objectives in environments where uncertainties and changes are sudden.

As when and how the changes will occur is not known, strategies cannot be composed according to a specific timetable. Creating strategy is an art, even if it can be defined by a specific process, as it does not have an accurate result.

2.2 Principles of Strategic Planning

Broadest participation must be ensured in strategic planning studies, and in this scope, employees from various units and levels of the business must be included in the planning process. Furthermore, the business will have the opportunity to know about itself as a whole by activating common mind, and as a by-product of this process, communication, and motivation within the business will be strengthened. As necessary, views must be received from other organizations and groups in the field of the business, to allow for a comprehensive status analysis. Basic principles are as follows:

- Each organization should
  - Consider its values, characteristics, structures and needs
  - Focus on contents rather than concepts
  - Develop its systematic of thinking
  - Introduce its definitions
  - Define its processes
- A radical climate of thinking should be created through brainstorming.
- A simple and mutual systematic of thinking must be adopted.
- Assumptions must be analyzed.
- It should be recognized that strategy development is a continuous process in nature.
- It should be understood that strategies are open to development and changes, but the systematic of strategic thinking is lasting.
- Participation must not be limited to senior management.

2.3 Forming a Planning Team

Support and orientation of senior management are indispensable conditions for strategic planning. Strategic planning team will execute the necessary work in communication with senior management and report the results. As necessary, it is possible to procure external consulting services.

It is critical that the planning team, which will take a crucial part in all steps of strategic planning, is created with a structure that serves the objectives, beginning from status analysis, for the success of these efforts:

- Are the key units of the business represented in the planning team?
- Do team members have the knowledge and skills required for strategic planning?
- Do team members have sufficient knowledge about the business?

- Do team members have sufficient knowledge about the target group or clients of the business?
- Can team members lend sufficient time and effort for strategic planning work?
- Can continuity be ensured in the team throughout the planning process?

3
STRATEGIC PLANNING APPROACH

3.1 Strategic Approach

Many models are developed regarding strategic planning. In periods when changes are sudden, static models do not provide significant benefit on creating competitive advantage due to the following reasons:

- The models developed do not encourage creative thinking due to their mechanic structure.
- Confusions arise on application, as the steps of the models and relations between these steps often cannot be defined as *process*.
- Despite concepts such as evaluation and application of strategy being mentioned on the developed strategic planning models, *strategy development* is not emphasized.

Questioning the assumptions and beliefs accepted by everyone within the organization and discussing which new opportunities could be created in case of the change of these beliefs is important.

While creating strategy, it should be accepted that anticipations based on experiences can also change. As creative thinking is distributed widely in each organization, it should not be monopoly of top management and occurrence of suppressed and isolated new and interesting perspectives should be provided.

In order to develop strategy, looking at the world with a new perspective and with a new objective, thinking of the facts in the simplest manner, and defining and examining according to these provides us to see the points that we are unable to see.

3.2 Development of Strategic Approach

It is necessary to consider the following factors in order to develop strategic approach. Figure 3.1 shows the factors of strategic approach.

Experience: In order to reveal different perspectives, it is necessary

- To benefit from the opinions of experienced individuals from the business or from outside.
- To arrange seminars, panel discussions, and meetings with these individuals.

Investigation: In order to accord with the changes in the environment in a short while, it will be right

- To adopt continuous learning as a philosophy within the business.
- To continuously renew the capital of information.
- To create an environment that questions and searches everything.

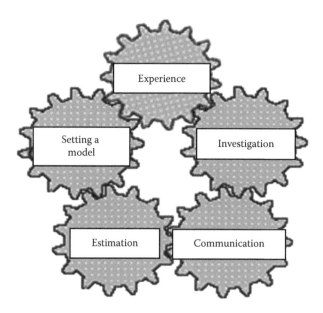

Figure 3.1   Factors of strategic approach.

Communication: In order to have information shared continuously, it is necessary

- To support team work.
- To extend participation and to give opportunity for the new participants of the business and for the ones working remote.
- To develop creative ideas by brainstorming sessions.

Estimation: In order to have continuous strategic progress, it is important

- To monitor the changes and developments regarding future.
- To compose visions regarding future.
- To make thinking about the future as a habit within the business.

Setting a model: The following are necessary within the business:

- The strategy should increase the value of business.
- Developing a *cash-flow model* peculiar to each condition should increase the value of business.
- Founding the cash-flow model on critical variables should increases the value of business.

4
FUNCTIONAL PLANS

A functional plan is the short-term plan for a key functional area within a company. Such plans clarify grand strategy by providing more specific details about how key functional areas are to be managed in the near future.

Functional plans help in the implementation of grand strategy by organizing and activating specific subunits of the company (marketing, financing, production, etc.) to pursue the business strategy in daily activities. They must be consistent with long-term objectives and grand strategy.

It is the responsibility of functional level managers to develop annual objectives and short-term plans in such areas as production, operations, and research and development; finance and accounting; marketing; and human relations. Figure 4.1 shows the basic functions and their contents.

However, their greatest responsibilities are in the implementation or execution of a company's strategic plan. While corporate and business-level managers center their planning concerns on doing the right things, managers at the functional level must stress doing things right. Thus, they directly address such issues as the efficiency and effectiveness of production and marketing systems, the quality and extent of customer service, and the success of particular products and services in increasing their market share. Basic characteristics are as follows:

- Formal and written plans
- Ties up business staff
- Must be justified as an investment
- Use different formats for different audiences
- Focus on ends rather than means
- Should cover contingency plans
- Should challenge assumptions

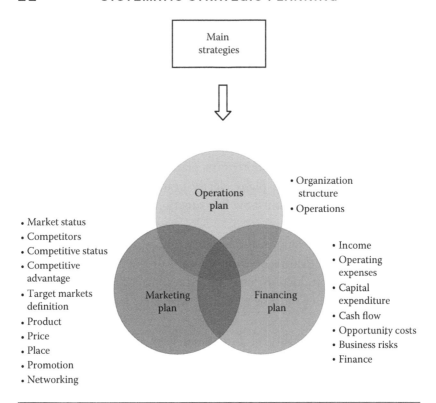

Figure 4.1   Basic functions and their contents. (A novel management diagram.)

4.1 Role of Functional Plans*

- Gathering and processing information include the following:
  - What are the customer's fundamental needs in relation to the product category?
  - What benefits does the product offer?
  - What problems do customers solve with the product?
  - How does the market currently serve to those needs?
  - What products are offered?
  - What features do they have?
  - In what ways does the market fail to serve those needs?
  - Why are customers left dissatisfied?
  - How often are they left dissatisfied?
  - How might customer needs be served better?
  - How might the product on offer be improved?

---

* Adapted from Wickham (2004).

- Organizing actions appropriate to pursuing the strategy are as follows:
  - How will the business address the needs of the customer?
  - How will demand be stimulated (e.g., communication, promotion, distribution, etc.?)
  - Why can the business deliver this in a way that competitors cannot?
  - What will be the competitive advantage that the business enjoys?
  - What are the competencies and capabilities of the business?
  - Why will competitors be unable to imitate them?
- Gaining stakeholders support.
- Definition of objectives and by calling upon formal project management techniques.

4.2 Marketing Plan

The role of marketing function is to profitably bring about the sale of products in target markets for the purpose of achieving the business's goals and being consistent with the grand strategy and other functional plans.

Effective marketing strategies guide marketing managers in determining who will sell what, where, to whom, in what quantity, and how.

Background to the market is* as follows:

- How the market is defined?
- Size of the market
- What is the total value of their sales?
- Major market sectors and niches
- Overall growth rate
- What shares of them are likely to be gained?
- How competitive will it be against existing products?
- Key trends in consumer behavior and buying habits

---

* Adapted from Wickham (2004).

- Technological developments in the product, service deliveries, and operations
- Over what period can the opportunity be exploited?
- How long will customers be interested?

Competitors and competitive conditions are[*] as follows:

- Key competitors with their strengths and weaknesses
- How long before competitors move in?
- Competitor's strategy and likely reaction to the business
- Basis of competition in the market
- Importance of price, product differentiation and branding
- Benefits to be gained from positioning

Definition of target market is[†] as follows:

- The way in which market is split up into different sectors.
- Dimensions of the market important for characterizing the sectors
- Market sectors that will be prioritized for targeting.

Product: A functional plan for the *product component* should guide marketing managers in decisions regarding features, product lines, packaging, accessories, warranty, quality, and new product development:

- What products will it compete with?
- How it will be differentiated from competitors in terms of features, quality, price, etc.?
- Which products contribute most to profitability?
- What is the product image we seek to project?
- What consumer needs does the product seek to meet?

Price: It directly influences demand and supply, profitability, consumer perception, and regulatory responses. The approach to pricing strategy may be cost oriented, market oriented, or competition oriented. With a cost-oriented approach, pricing decisions center on total cost and usually involve an acceptable markup or target price ranges. Pricing is based on consumer demand when the approach is

---

[*] Adapted from Wickham (2004).
[†] Adapted from Wickham (2004).

market oriented. With the third approach, pricing decisions center on those of the firm's competitors.

- What is the unit cost likely to be?
- How much will customers pay for the product?
- Are we primarily competing on price?
- Are pricing policies standard nationally or is there regional control?
- What price segments are we targeting (high, medium, low, etc.)?

Place: The functional plan for the *place component* identifies where, when, and by whom the product are to be offered for sale. The primary concern here is the channels(s) of distribution—the combination of marketing institutions through which the products flow to the final user to ensure consistency with the total marketing effort.

- Intermediaries (wholesalers, distributors, retailers) and strategies for them.
- What level of market coverage is necessary?
- Are there priority geographic areas?
- What are the channel objectives, structure, and management?
- Should the marketing managers change their degree of reliance on distributors, sales reps, and direct selling?
- What sales organization do we want?
- Is the sales force organized around territory, market, or product?

Promotion: It defines how the firm will communicate with the target market. Functional plan for the *promotion component* should provide marketing managers with basic guides for the use and mix of advertising, personal selling, sales promotion, and media selection. It must be consistent with other marketing strategy components and, due to cost requirements, closely integrated with financial plan.

- Is the sales force organized around territory, market or product?
- Sales and price promotions
- Public relations activity

- What are key promotion priorities and approaches?
- Which advertising/communication priorities and approaches are linked to different products, markets, and territories?

Networking

4.3 Operations Plan

Functional plans in operations must guide decisions regarding (1) an optimum balance between investment input and production/operations output and (2) location, facilities design, and process planning on a short-term basis.

The facilities and equipment component of operations strategy involves decisions regarding plant location, size, equipment, replacement, and facilities utilization that should be consistent with grand strategy and other operating plans.

Functional plans for the planning and control component of operations provide guidelines for ongoing production operations. They are meant to encourage efficient organization of production/operations resources to match long-range, overall demand. Often this component dictates whether production/operations will be demand oriented, inventory oriented, or subcontracted oriented.

Operations plan must be coordinated with marketing plan if the firm is to succeed. Careful integration with financial plan components (such as capital budgeting and investment decisions) and the personnel function are also necessary.

Personnel management aids in accomplishing grand strategy by ensuring the development of managerial talent, and the development of competent, well-motivated employees. Functional plans in the personnel area are needed to guide decisions regarding compensation, labor relations, etc.

Organization structure
It includes the following:

- Roles and responsibilities
- Relationships among positions
- Skills and experiences, personal profiles, estimated salaries, etc.

- Employee recruitment, selection, and orientation
- Career development and counseling, performance evaluation, and training and development
- Labor/union relations
- Discipline, control, and evaluation
- What are the key human resource needs to support a chosen strategy?
- How do we recruit for these needs?
- How sophisticated should the selection process be?
- How should new employees be introduced to the organization?

Operations

- Planned amount of production per month one year
- Cost estimates on the facilities, equipment
- How centralized should the facilities be? (One big facility or several small facilities?)
- How integrated should the separate processes be?
- To what extent will further mechanization or automation be pursued?
- Should size and capacity be oriented toward peak or normal operating levels?
- How many purchasing sources are needed?
- How do we select suppliers and manage relationships over time?
- What level of forward buying (hedging) is appropriate?
- Should work be scheduled to order or to stock?
- What level of inventory is appropriate?
- How should inventory be used (FIFO, LIFO), controlled, and replenished?
- What are the key factors for control efforts (quality, labor cost, downtime, product usage, other)?
- What emphasis should be placed on job specialization? Plant safety? Use of standards?
- What level of productivity is critical?
- How far ahead should we schedule production? Guarantee delivery? Hire personnel?
- What criteria should be followed in adding or deleting equipment, facilities, shifts, and people?

4.4 Financing Plan

Financing plans guide financial managers in long-term capital investment, use of debt financing, dividend allocation, and the business' leveraging posture. Financing plans designed to manage working capital and short term assets have a more immediate focus.

Long-term financing plans usually guide capital acquisition in the sense that priorities change infrequently over time. Another financing plan of major importance is capital allocation. Growth-oriented main strategies generally require numerous major investments in facilities, projects, acquisitions, and/or people. This helps manage conflicting priorities among operating managers competing for capital resources. A clear financial strategy that sets capital allocation priorities is important for effective implementation.

Capital allocation strategy frequently includes another dimension level of capital expenditure delegated to operating managers. If a business is pursuing a rapid growth, flexibility in making capital expenditures at the operating level may enable timely responses to an evolving market. On the other hand, capital expenditures may be carefully controlled if retrenchment is the strategy.

Dividend management is an integral part of a business' internal financing. Lower dividends increase the internal funds available for growth, and internal financing reduces the need for external, often debt, financing.

Working capital requirement analysis is critical to the daily operation of the business, and capital requirements are directly influenced by seasonal and cyclical fluctuations, business size, and pattern of receipts and disbursements.

Income:

- What profits will be generated?
- Over what period?
- Is this attractive given the investment necessary?
- How does return on investment compare to other investment options?

Operating expenses:

- Expenditures on labor, raw materials, energy, and consumables
- Financial expenses

Capital expenditure:

- What are the immediate capital requirements?
- What investments in people, operating assets, and communication will be required to start the business?
- What will be the long-term and ongoing capital requirements?
- What future investments will be necessary to continue exploiting the opportunity?
- Does the business have access to the capital required?
- If the opportunity is as large as expected, will the business have sufficient capacity?
- If not, can it be expanded or be profitably offset to other organizations?
- What human resources will be needed?
- Are they available?

Business risks*:

The following are included in the business risks:

- How sound are the assumptions about the size of the opportunity?
- How accurate was the data on markets?
- How all competitor products been considered?
- What if customers do not find the offering as attractive as expected?
- What if competitors are more responsive than expected?
- Have all competitors been considered?
- How could they react in principle?
- How might they react in practice?
- To what extent is success dependent on the support and goodwill of intermediaries and other third parties?
- How will this goodwill be gained and maintained?
- How sensitive will the exploitation be to the marketing strategy?
- Are there formations risking profitability in the trends of the industry?
- What are the factors imperative for success?

---

* Adapted from Wickham (2004).

- Are external factors likely to affect profitability?
- Is it possible to take measures to eliminate the risks identified?
- Can adjustments be made to the strategy in the light of experience?
- How expensive will this be?
- Can additional resources be made available if necessary?
- Will these be from internal sources or from investors?
- What will be the effect on cash flow if revenues are lower than expected?
- What will be the effect on cash flow if costs are higher than expected?
- How should investors be prepared for these eventualities?
- How should future revenues be discounted?
- Under what circumstances might investors wish to make an exit?
- Will this be planned or in response to a crisis?

Finance:

- What is an acceptable cost of capital?
- What is the desired proportion of short-term and long-term debt: preferred and common equity?
- What balance is between internal and external funding?
- What risk and ownership restrictions are appropriate?
- What level of capital allocation can be made by operating managers without higher approval?
- What are the priorities for capital allocation projects?
- On what basis is final selection of projects to be made?
- What portion of earnings should be made paid capital management out as dividends?
- How important is dividend stability?
- Are things other than cash flow requirements; minimum and maximum cash balances?
- How liberal/conservative should credit policies be?
- What limits, payment terms, and collection procedures are necessary?
- What payment timing and procedure should be followed?

PART II
Systematic Strategic Planning (SSP)

Systematic Strategic Planning is the pattern of procedures by which an organization defines its current status, opportunities, long-term goals, and the strategies for which to achieve them. SSP is based on the principles of $P \times D$ (*Planning by Design*), which is generated by Muther (2011).

The aim of systematic strategic planning is to force a look into the future and therefore provides an opportunity to influence the future, or assume a proactive posture, to provide better awareness of needs and environment, to help define and focus on the objectives of the organization, to provide a sense of direction, continuity, and effective leadership and to plug everyone into the system and provides standards of accountability for people, programs, and allocated resources.

Full and shortened versions will be reviewed in the following chapters, as two different planning models.

The techniques to be used for strategic planning should not be perceived as a procedure of systematic, and the techniques used should be continuously repeatable and modifiable depending on the characteristics of individual cases.

Certain working forms (in the forms of key documents and output) are used in applying the techniques in each section or steps of the SSP pattern.

5

SSP

Full Version

Systematic strategic planning—full version consists of a framework of phases through which each project passes, a pattern of sections for straight-forward planning, and the fundamentals involved in any strategic planning project. Figure 5.1 illustrates SSP full version.

5.1 SSP: Four Phases

Each strategic planning project has four phases. These are as follows:

- *Phase I*: Orientation
- *Phase II*: Overall (Corporate) strategic plan
- *Phase III*: Detailed (Business) strategic plans
- *Phase IV*: Implementation plan and control

In Phases II and III, the planning specialist follows a method of procedures to achieve alternative strategic plans.

In holdings/large businesses, planning specialist uses Phase II in full SSP version to develop overall strategic plan. Planning specialist may repeat Phase III of the full version to develop detailed strategic plans of each business/division of the holding/large business, or may use shortened SSP version instead if the business is small.

5.1.1 Orientation

In this phase, understand the objective(s) of the assignment—its purpose, goals, priorities, or requirements. The external conditions are determined—basic assumptions or other surrounding legal, financial, technological, political, organizational, or economic constraints to be related with. The planning situation is clarifying—who is responsible for doing what by when; where to work; others involved; any mandatory aspects of the assignment or any constraints under which the

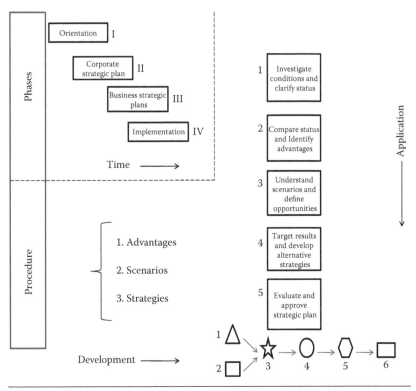

Figure 5.1   SSP—reference table.

planning is to be done. The scope is determined, the extents or boundaries of the planning (Appendix D – Orientation Worksheet.)

Furthermore, questions to encourage creative thinking about the organization under review are prepared. For example, these questions may be intended to identify the changes in the expectations and priorities of clients to draw a picture of the future of the organization, the competitive environment, domestic and international trends in the industry. It is important that the questions are prepared in such a manner that a Brainstorming environment (Appendix B) will be created to the extent possible.

Particular attention must be paid to ensure that a comfortable and informal working environment, freed from day-to-day procedures, is created. In order to objectively collect the information about the organization under review, experienced individuals outside the organization but from among stakeholders (e.g., suppliers, clients, vendors, etc.) are identified. In addition, relevant knowledgeable and participatory individuals are identified from the organization (regardless of hierarchy).

5.1.2 Overall (Corporate) Strategic Plan

Here, corporate represents a group of businesses or a large business consisting of various divisions. For example, for a group of businesses active in various industries, a comprehensive and overall strategic plan must be handled in this phase.

Corporate strategic plan is a document that provides guidance for the employees, and information for stakeholders through its high-level statement of how we propose to go about our work over the next three to five years. The method forming the sections required for Phase II is explained in detail in the following section.

5.1.3 Detailed (Business) Strategic Plans

It is the phase in which separate strategic plans are prepared for each business or division. It ensures that strategic plans at the level of businesses are aligned and integrated with overall strategic plan. The method forming the sections required for Phase III is also explained in the following section.

5.1.4 Implementation Plan and Control

The implementation plan is a tool that gets corporate and businesses strategic plans underway. It is set of activities design to achieve the objectives of the project. Implementation plan is about how organization reaches objectives that are determined in strategic plans. In implementation plan, organizations decide that where, how, when, and whom actions are done.

Furthermore, performance criteria are monitored in this phase, to identify deviations from goals and analyze the reasons of these deviations. In case the desired goals cannot be achieved, the plan is modified or a new plan is prepared according to the suggestions of solution to be produced. This phase is explained in detail in Part IV.

5.2 SSP: Three Fundamentals

The fundamentals of strategic planning—and therefore, the basis on which any strategic planning must rest—are *competitive advantages, scenarios, and strategies.*

5.2.1 Competitive Advantages

Competitive advantages are fundamental A. As a result of investigating internal and external factors, weaknesses and strengths of the organization determined. Based on the comparison of the strengths with market conditions, the unique strengths, that is, competitive advantages of the organization are determined.

5.2.2 Scenarios

Scenarios are fundamental B. Scenario analysis is made on external factors—macroeconomic analysis, industry analysis, etc. By this analysis, negative and positive scenarios are determined. These scenarios help to predict the industry's future.

5.2.3 Strategies

Strategies are fundamental C. Strategies are the fundamental that helps the organization to define how to reach to the opportunity (that is brought out by matching fundamental A [i.e., competitive advantage] with fundamental B [i.e., scenarios]). This fundamental characterizes the process that organization should follow in order to reach the opportunity and guides the organization about how it should be done.

5.3 SSP: Five Sections

Phase II and III passes through the following five sections. Figure 5.2 illustrates the five sections of SSP.

5.3.1 Investigating Environmental and Internal Conditions: Clarification of Current Status

The first section of strategic planning systematic is to answer the question, "where are we?" This requires a comprehensive status analysis. Status analysis essentially covers the following assessments:

- Analysis of the internal structure of the organization (analysis of the duties and authorities, performances, problems, potentials, institutional culture, human resources, technology level, etc. of the organization.)

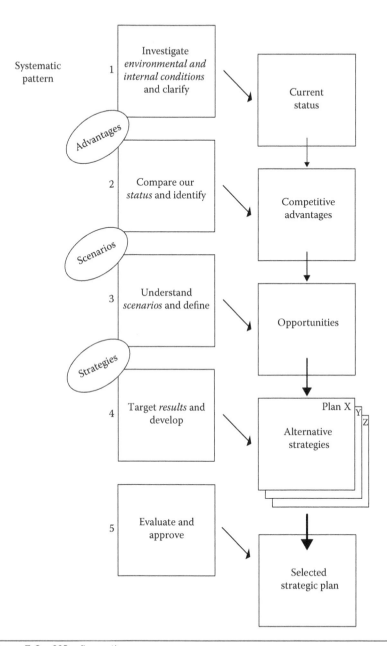

Figure 5.2 SSP—five sections.

- Environmental analysis (analysis of external conditions as well as the environment in which the organization operates and related parties—target group of the organization and parties affected negatively/positively from the organization's activities.)
- Analysis of developments that the organization may face and be affected in the future.

While making these assessments, the global and domestic trends in the sector/subsector in which the organization operates are discussed.

During and after status analysis, the internal strengths and weaknesses of the organization and developments originating from the external factors are identified.

5.3.2 Comparison of Status and Identification of Competitive Advantages

The organization's strengths and weaknesses are compared with the key factors in the market development phases, capacities and resources of main competitors and the industry's success factors, to identify competitive advantages.

5.3.3 Understand Scenarios and Define Opportunities

Forecasts are made regarding the future changes in the field of business in which the organization operates, or plans to operate in the future; for example, in what direction customer needs and expectations will evolve and develop in the future.

First of all, the scenarios to be created by trends revealed by environmental analysis for the industry must be developed; that is, alternative scenarios must be developed for the future.

In order to promote various ideas during this section, seminars, panels or brainstorming meetings must be organized with experts having relevant knowledge and experience, both within and outside the organization.

The opportunities and threats that may be offered and posed for the organization by positive and negative scenarios revealed by scenario analysis must be identified. Furthermore, identification of the organization's competitive advantages and weaknesses relative to competitors and industry standards could lead this section to an efficient result. In short, in order to identify opportunities and threats, the organization's competitive advantages and weaknesses must be matched with potential positive (attractive) and negative (risky) scenarios that may be encountered in the industry.

5.3.4 *Identification of Strategic Objectives and Main Goals and Development of Alternative Strategies*

Strategic objectives are the conceptual results which the organization aims at achieving within a certain period of time. Strategic objectives and goals answer the organization's question, "what do we want to achieve?" in the strategic planning systematic.

Main goals are the specific and measurable subobjectives established for the achievement of strategic objectives. Unlike strategic objectives, goals are expressed quantitatively and cover a shorter term. Multiple goals may be set to achieve a strategic objective. For example,

- Operational goals
- Marketing goals
- Financial goals

Strategies are instruments ensuring the achievement of long-term goals. It is a course of action selected from a series of options in order to achieve a goal establish against uncertainties. It is critical to distinguish between goals and strategies. Goals imply the desired result. Strategy, however, shows how the goal can be achieved.

For the organization to achieve a lasting competitive advantage in its own industry and markets, it searches for answers to the question, "what should be done?" and develops alternative strategies. So, it is necessary to analyze what should be done and how should they be done to attain opportunities and thus achieve goals, as well as to identify alternative strategies. For example,

- Differentiation
- Focusing
- Cost leadership

5.3.5 *Evaluating Strategic Plans and Selecting the Best*

Here, the strategic plan most suitable for the organization can be selected. To do this, you make an evaluation of the alternatives based on qualitative factors. For example,

- Synergy
- Competitive advantages
- Flexible organization structure
- Market orientation
- Critical success factors

Furthermore, it is necessary to evaluate the profitability of alternative strategy and the risk elements from which it may be affected (mainly labor force, management, client, etc.) and to identify the probability of

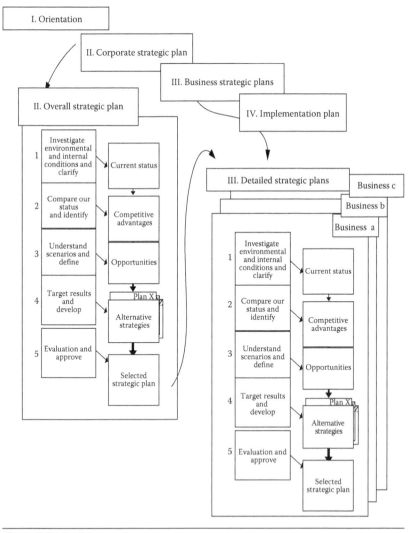

Figure 5.3   Sections repeat.

its actualization within the plan. Hence, alternative strategies should be listed from the least risky to most risky (considering their probability of actualization.)

Thus, the most suitable strategic plan is selected by evaluating them according to qualitative factors and considering potential risk factors.

5.3.6 *Sections Repeat*

The sections of full SSP version are repeated in Phases II and III. The sections are applied once during Phase II, to develop *overall strategic plan*. Then, the sections are repeated in Phase III for each business/division (as shown in Figure 5.3).

6
SSP

Shortened Version

Shortened Systematic Strategic Planning consists of six steps only. Figure 6.1 illustrates the shortened version of SSP. Planning specialist may combine Phases II and III under the *Shortened SSP* version, which is shorter. Phase IV is defined as Step 6 in the shortened SSP version.

A strategic plan includes the fundamentals *competitive advantages*, *scenarios*, and *strategies* as discussed in Chapter 5. Shortened SSP constitutes a six-step method intended to identify these three fundamentals.

Part III explains the first five steps, and Part IV explains step 6 in detail.

The use of shortened SSP version is more suitable for the development of strategic plans for small- and medium-size businesses (SMEs).

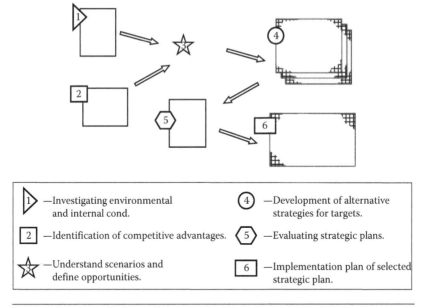

Figure 6.1   Shortened systematic strategic planning.

PART III

Systematic Strategic Planning Sections

The next five chapters take us through the SSP pattern. Figure III.1 shows the systematic pattern of SSP. They describe step-by-step the procedure and techniques of analysis to be used. Each chapter is devoted to a specific section of the pattern.

Note that the chapters in Part III discuss pattern of procedures that are essentially the same for both Phases II and III. The pattern merely repeats itself for each of the business in Phase III.

For the purpose of this book, the term business is used as a generic term for representing the organizations mentioned at the level of Phases II or III.

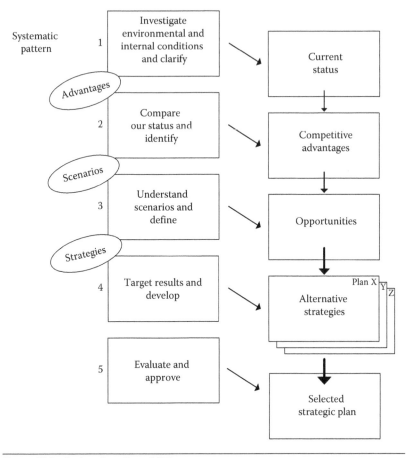

Figure III.1   Systematic pattern of SSP.

7

ENVIRONMENTAL AND INTERNAL ANALYSIS

Current Status

The first section of strategic systematic planning is to answer the question "where are we?" This requires a comprehensive status analysis. Status analysis essentially covers the following assessments:

- Analysis of the internal structure of the organization (analysis of the duties and authorities, performances, problems, potentials, institutional culture, human resources, technology level, etc., of the organization.)
- Environmental analysis (analysis of external conditions as well as the environment in which the organization operates and related parties—target group of the organization and parties affected negatively or positively from the organization's activities.)
- Analysis of developments that the organization may face and be affected by in the future.

Status analysis begins with a short history of the business and lays down the policies followed and performance demonstrated by the business during recent years within the framework of its mission. Thus, the conformity of goods and/or services produced by the business to the overall goals and policies, how the business serves its target group, the general strategies adopted in this respect, etc., are assessed. While making these assessments, the global and domestic trends in the sector/subsector in which the business operates are discussed.

The analysis of factors within and outside the control of the business and the factors that cause uncertainties constitute an important part of status analysis. During and after status analysis, the internal strengths and weaknesses of the business and the developments originating from external factors are identified.

While performing intrabusiness assessment and environmental analysis, the negativities and uncertainties which the business may face are particularly identified and evaluated during the subsequent sections of strategic systematic planning.

Instruments like documentation review, interview, survey, and similar studies, and participatory meetings bringing together various groups concerning the business are used while performing status analysis. For the efforts to be made in this scope, it is possible to outsource specialized services, such as the use of facilitators (moderators) who will neutrally facilitate participatory meetings.

The findings obtained as a result of status analysis are reported systematically, evaluated by responsible individuals and teams, and used in the further phases of the planning process. Detailed documents of status analysis may be provided in the appendix of strategic plan as necessary.

7.1 Internal Analysis

While an internal status analysis, which is illustrated in Figure 7.1, is performed within the business, the past performance of business is evaluated as well as its strengths and weaknesses are put forth. The purpose is to identify the potential of the business taking into consideration its existing performance and problems. The strengths to be identified will throw light on the future goals of the business, whereas its weaknesses will form the basis of the measures to be taken by the

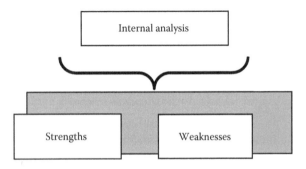

Figure 7.1   Internal analysis.

business. Strengths and weaknesses of the business ascertained within the framework of these studies are outlined in a summary table.

This is accomplished by identifying and then evaluating strategic internal factors. What are strategic internal factors? Where do they originate? How do we decide which are the truly strategic factors that must be carefully evaluated? These questions might be raised by managers in identifying and then evaluating key internal factors as strengths or weaknesses on which to base the business' strategy.

7.1.1 Functional Approach

Strategic internal factors are a business' basic capabilities, limitations, and characteristics. In Section 7.1.3, typical factors, some of which would be the focus of internal analysis in most businesses, are listed. This list of factors is broken down along functional lines.

Diagnosing a business' key strengths and weaknesses requires the adoption of a disaggregated view of the business. Examining the business across distinct functional areas, as suggested earlier is one way to disaggregate the business for internal analysis purposes. Table 7.1 is a worksheet that can be used for functional approach.

Therefore, the business should examine past performance to isolate key internal contributors to favorable (or unfavorable) results. What did we do well, or poorly, in sales operations, and financial operations, and financial management that had a major influence on past results? Was the sales force effectively organized? Were we in the right channels of distribution? Did we have the financial resources to support the past strategy? Table 7.2 illustrates an example on a business history summary worksheet. The same examination and questions can be applied to business' current situation, with a particular emphasis on changes in the importance of key dimensions over time.

For example, analysis of past trends in sales, costs, and profitability is of major importance in identifying strategic internal factors. An anatomy of past trends broken down by product lines, channels of distribution, key customers or types of customers, geographic region, sales approach, etc., should be developed in detail. A business may determine that certain key internal factors (e.g., experience in particular distribution channels, pricing policies, warehouse location, and technology) deserve major attention in formulating future strategy.

Table 7.1   Functional Approach

	FACTORS	STRENGTHS/WEAKNESSES
Marketing	Firm's products/services; breadth of product line	
	Concentration of sales in a few products or to a few customers	
	Ability to gather needed information about markets	
	Market share or submarket shares	
	Product/service mix and expansion potential	
	Channels of distribution: number, coverage, and control	
	Effective sales organization	
	Product/service image, reputation, and quality	
	Imaginative, efficient and effective sales promotion and advertising	
	Pricing strategy and pricing flexibility	
	Procedures for digesting market feedback and developing new products, services or markets	
	Aftersale service and follow-up	
	Goodwill/brand loyalty	
Finance and Accounting	Ability to raise short-term capital	
	Ability to raise long-term capital: debt/equity	
	Corporate-level resources	
	Cost of capital relative to industry and competitors	
	Tax considerations	
	Relations with owners, investors, and stockholders	
	Leverage positions	
	Cost of entry and barriers to entry	
	Price–earnings ratio	
	Working capital; flexibility of capital structure	
	Effective cost control, ability to reduce costs	
	Financial size	
	Efficient and effective accounting system for cost, budget and profit planning	
Production/ Operations/ Technical	Raw materials cost and availability	
	Inventory control systems; inventory turnover	
	Location of facilities; layout and utilization of facilities	
	Economies of scale	

(*Continued*)

Table 7.1 (*Continued*)   Functional Approach

	FACTORS	STRENGTHS/WEAKNESSES
	Technical efficiency of facilities and utilization of capacity	
	Effective use of subcontracting	
	Degree of vertical integration, value added and profit margin	
	Efficiency and cost/benefit of equipment	
	Effective operation control procedures	
	Cost and technological competencies relative to industry and competitors	
	Research and development/technology/innovation	
	Patents, trademarks, and similar legal protection	
Personnel	Management personnel	
	Employees' skill and morale	
	Labor relations compared to industry and competition	
	Efficient and effective personnel policies	
	Effective use of incentives to motivate performance	
	Ability to level peaks and valleys of employment	
	Employee turnover and absenteeism	
	Specialized skills	
	Experience	
Organization and General Management	Organizational structure	
	Firm's image and prestige	
	Firm's record for achieving objectives	
	Organization of communication system	
	Overall organizational control system	
	Organizational climate, culture	
	Use of systematic procedures and techniques in decision making	
	Top-management skill, capacities, and interest	
	Strategic planning system	
	Intraorganizational synergy	

Numerous quantitative tools are available for evaluating selected internal capabilities of a business. These entail measurement of a business' effectiveness vis-a-vis each relevant factor and comparative analysis of this measurement against the historical experience of the business. Ratio analysis is useful for evaluating, selected financial, sales, and operating factors. The business' balance sheet and income

Table 7.2 Business History Summary—Manufacturing Business X

	YEAR	YEAR	YEAR	YEAR	YEAR
Personnel	No. of employees: 2, 1 clerk, 1 labor	No. of employees: 28, 14 clerks, 14 labors	No. of employees: 39, 21 clerks, 18 labors	No. of employees: 39, 21 clerks, 18 labors	No. of employees: 48, 27 clerks, 21 labors
Technical		Lime production	Cement-based ready-made plaster plant investment and production	Gypsum production plant investment: know-how outsourced mechanically applied gypsum-based plaster production	Gypsum-based plaster plant investment (all investment made with own know-how)
Organization and General Management	Established				
Production/Operations			Plaster machine imports and leasing to practitioner headquarters moved to a larger building	Vatering and maintenance activities subcontracted	
Marketing		Two products (lime)	Cement-based plaster and lime sales number of products offered to market: six direct sales system	Number of products offered to market: eight	
Finance and Accounting (×1000)	Turnover profitability capital	Turnover profit. capital	Turnover profiatability capital	Turnover profitability capital	

statements are important sources from which to derive meaning-ful ratios. Examples of other quantitative or analytical tools include cash flow analysis, sensitivity analysis, and elasticity and variability analysis.

Quantitative tools cannot be applied to all internal factors, and the judgments of the key planning participants may be used in evaluation. Company or product image and prestige are examples of internal factors more appropriate to qualitative evaluation.

7.1.2 Value-Added Approach*

Another way to disaggregate the business is to use a framework called the *value chain* (Porter 1998). A value chain is a systematic way of viewing the series of activities a business performs to provide a product to its customers.

Every business can be viewed as a collection of value functions that are performed to design, produce, market, deliver, and support its products. These functions can be grouped into nine basic categories, within each category, functions represent key strengths or weaknesses of the business. Through the systematic identification of these discrete functions, managers using the value chain approach can target potential strengths and weaknesses for further evaluation.

7.1.2.1 Primary Functions   Primary functions are those involved in the physical creation of the business' product or service, its delivery, and sales to the buyer, and its aftersale support. Overarching each of these are support functions, which provide inputs or infrastructure allowing the primary functions to take place on an ongoing basis. Identifying primary functions requires the isolation of functions that are technologically and strategically distinct. Each of the five basic categories is divisible into several distinct functions:

- *Inbound logistics*: Functions associated with receiving, storing, and disseminating inputs to the product, such as material handling, warehousing, inventory control, vehicle scheduling, and returns to suppliers.

---

* Adapted from Porter (1998).

- *Operations*: Functions associated with transforming inputs into the final product form, such as machining, packaging, assembly, equipment maintenance, testing, printing, and facility operations.
- *Outbound logistics*: Functions associated with collecting, storing, and physically distributing the product to buyers, such as finished goods warehousing, material handling, delivery vehicle operation, order processing, and scheduling.
- *Marketing and sales*: Functions associated with providing a means by which buyers can purchase the product and inducing them to do so, such as advertising, promotion, sales force, quoting, channel selection, channel relations, and pricing.
- *Service*: Functions associated with providing service to enhance or maintain the value of the product, such as installation, repair, training, parts supply, and product adjustment.

The primary functions depend on the particular industry. For example, for a food distributor, inbound and outbound logistics are the most critical areas. After sales, service is becoming increasingly critical to automotive dealerships. Yet, all the primary functions are present to some degree and deserve attention in a systematic internal analysis.

7.1.2.2 Support Functions   Support value functions arise in one of four categories and can be identified or disaggregated by isolating technologically or strategically distinct functions. These four areas can typically be distinguished as follows:

1. *Procurement*: Functions involved in obtaining purchased inputs, whether raw materials, purchased services, machinery, or so on. Procurement stretches across the entire value chain because it supports every function—every function uses purchased inputs of some kind. Many discrete functions are typically performed within a business, often by different people.
2. *Technology development*: Functions involved in designing the product as well as in creating and improving the way the various functions in the value chain are performed. We tend to

think of technology in terms of the product or manufacturing process. In fact, every function a business performs involves a technology or technologies, which may be sophisticated, and a business has a stock of know-how for performing each function. Technology development typically involves a variety of discrete functions, some performed outside the R&D department.

3. *Human resource management*: Functions necessary to ensure the recruiting, training, and development of personnel. Every function involves human resources, and thus human resource management functions cut across the entire chain.

4. *Business infrastructure*: Such functions as general management, accounting, legal, finance, strategic planning, and all others decoupled from specific primary or support functions but essential to the entire chain's operation.

The value chain provides a useful approach to guide a systematic internal analysis of the business' existing or potential strengths and weaknesses. Disaggregating a business into nine function categories, the business has identified key internal factors for further examination as potential sources of competitive advantage. In this approach, it is important to correctly figure out the organization's

- Value-added chain
- Functions
- Process flow charts demonstrating the linkages between value-added chain and functions

1. This starts with the definition of the business:
   - What is being done in the organization? Production, marketing, distribution, purchasing, etc.
   - Creation of process flow charts: How and for what purpose are operations performed? The processes within the rings making up the value-added chain and the process flow charts constituting these processes. For example, process of the product sold from the warehouse and its shipment, or various processes during production stage, etc.
   - Analysis of the organization chart: Where and by whom are the operations performed? Review of departments and functions of departments, assignment of employees, positions of departments, job descriptions, and characteristics, etc.

2. Definition of the organization's functions:
   - Making the business definition
   - Determination of value chain
   - Determination of processes composing the rings of the chain and of work flow schemes
   - Expansion of processes and flow schemes and definition of work units
   - Determination of parameters and variables affecting the work units
   - Determination of the effects of these variables on the expense and profit centers
   - Grouping and consolidation of variables according to their effects
   - Determination of relations among expense and profit centers by processes and their schemes

3. Definition of the organization's structure:
   - Evaluation of the organization's scheme. Comparison of the organization's scheme, work groups, and positions and the functions of the organization.
   - Business groups of each department to the lowest levels and its development to define the work units.
   - Making job and duty definitions on the basis of work unit.
   - Determination of characteristics required for each work unit and position.
   - Determination of variables affecting these characteristics.
   - Determination of the position that is most affected by each variable.
   - Grouping and consolidation of variables according to their impacts.
   - Determination of relations among positions on the flow schemes.

4. Analysis of variables and critical processes:
   - Examination of correlation among the variables determined as a result of the evaluation of value chain and organization scheme, and grouping the ones that are related to each other.
   - Determination of parameters that are measurable and that can be expressed numerically. Separating and grouping

the ones that can be and cannot be expressed numerically as dependent and independent variables.
- Composition of relations matrix and examination of the relations among all the variables.
- Determination of variables that affect others at most but that are not affected by any variable within the organization and that are out of the control of the organization (external variables).
- Determination of variables that affect the others at most but that are not affected from any variable outside the organization (internal variables).
- Aligning the variables that are considered to affect each expense and profit center at most in the order of significance and composition of value effect matrix.
- According to the composed value effect matrix, laying out the processes and work flow schemes where each variable exists.
- Determination of critical processes that will compose in case of having variables that have correlation with each other and that have high effect within the same processes.
- In order to determine the aforementioned issues, for example, the following questions are required to be answered starting from the lowest level of the organization and as objective as possible considering the current work flows and the organization's structure and the answers shall be evaluated by a higher level.

5. Thus, critical processes where company performances cannot be expressed numerically will be revealed as follows:
   - What are we doing?
   - What do we do best?
   - What can't we do best?
   - Where do we want to be?

7.1.3 Strengths and Weaknesses of Business

The considerations revealed by *Functional* or *Value-Added* approach are grouped under various functional headings such as overall management, human resources, operations/technology, marketing, finance and accounting, and their distinction as things done well or poorly. Table 7.3 illustrates an example of a business strengths and weaknesses worksheet:

Organization and general management:

- Rate of deviation in the implementation of strategic plans
- Organizational structure
- Business image and prestige
- Communication system
- Organization control system (productivity and resource utilization)
- Organizational culture
- Decision-making mechanisms
- Synergy and collaboration within the organization
- Senior management skills, educational status
- Political power of senior managers
- Tendencies of senior managers to work as a team

Personnel:

- Staff management
- Employee–employer relations within the industry
- Efficient and effective staff regulations
- Efficiency of incentives to improve performance
- Skills and morale of employees
- Experience
- Employee costs
- Employee turnover rate
- Career planning
- Level of wages relative to the market

Production/operations/technical:

- Raw-materials cost/supplier relations
- Inventory control system/inventory turnover rate
- Location/layout of the facility
- Economies of scale
- Building and equipment

Table 7.3   Business Strengths and Weaknesses—Manufacturing Business X

	STRENGTHS	WEAKNESSES
Organization and General Management	1. Flexible and horizontal relations facilitate decision making 2. Participatory and sharing management 3. Broad investment vision 4. Prestigious company name 5. Experienced management staff undertaking responsibilities 6. Strategic planning and budget discipline	1. Lack of continuity in organization 2. Corporate culture not matured 3. Instant decision making, quick giving up of decisions taken
Personnel	1. Competent, experienced, and responsible staff 2. Qualified and young labor force 3. Specialized staff	1. Motivational instruments lacking 2. High employee turnover rate 3. No career plan 4. Stressful environment, fatigue factor
Production/ Operations/ Technical	1. Ease of raw material supply 2. Good suppliers relations 3. Registered trademarks 4. Effective use of subcontractors 5. Production control procedures applied 7. Effective quality control 8. Vertical integration 9. Technical team competence 10. Product development capacity 11. Development potential of products	1. Layouts disorganized in production units 2. No R&D investment, no budgeting 3. Single-site production and distribution channel 4. Low-capacity utilization
Marketing	1. Product diversity 2. Market leader 3. Presales application service 4. Qualification and competence in distribution channels 5. Quality and branded products 6. Technical support department 7. Strong references 8. Postsales support	1. Limited product range 2. Sales concentrated on specific products and customers 3. Collection of information about the industry depends on personal competencies 4. Distribution channels insufficient in technical and sophisticated products 5. Lack of sales organization 6. Product image and familiarity low in technical and sophisticated products 7. Marketing activities insufficient 8. Lack of customer relations management

(Continued)

Table 7.3 (*Continued*) Business Strengths and Weaknesses—Manufacturing Business X

	STRENGTHS	WEAKNESSES
Finance and Accounting	1. Automation and integration through system investments 2. Effective cost control 3. High credibility 4. Positive relations with shareholders, strong shareholding structure 5. High equity profitability 6. High working capital ratio 7. High profit margin 8. Long-term capital raising capacity 9. Image of a tax paying and strong company	1. Investments financed totally from own resources 2. Claims collection time longer than debt payment time 3. Inventory management 4. Sales not collateralized

- Capacity utilization and productivity
- Quality certificates and awards received
- Efficient use of subcontractors
- Degree of vertical integration—value added
- Cost-potential study of equipments and productivity
- Effective operational control procedures
- Costs and technical qualification relative to the industry
- Research and development/technology/innovation
- Patent, trademark, and similar legal protections

Marketing:

- Products/product range
- Focus on product or customer in sales
- Ability to gather information about the market
- Market share
- Mixed production program and potential expansion
- Life cycle of primary products
- Product profit/sales balance
- Ability to control distribution channels
- Efficient sales organization
- Knowledge of customer needs
- Product image, prestige, and quality
- Creativity

- Productive and effective sales promotion and advertisement
- Pricing strategy and pricing flexibility
- Market feedback
- Ability to follow up emerging products or markets
- Postsales service and monitoring program
- Value of business/brand loyalty

Finance and accounting:

- Capacity to create short-term capital
- Capacity to create long-term capital
- Corporate-level resources
- Capital cost in the industry
- Comments and ideas about taxation
- Relations with owners, investors, and shareholders
- Capacity to utilize alternative finance
- Entry cost and entry barriers
- Price–profit ratio
- Working capital/flexibility of capital composition
- Efficient cost control/ability to reduce costs
- Efficient and effective accounting system

7.2 Environmental Analysis

Intention of environmental analysis:

- To determine the developments and trends in the macroeconomic (demographical, economical, judicial–political, technological, sociocultural) environment that effects the business and its industry at most
- To understand the powers that effect competition in the industry (new businesses, customers, suppliers, substitutes, competitors, government, financial institutions, etc.)
- To anticipate the trends that these powers could create for the industry

Environmental analysis, which is illustrated in Figure 7.2, considers the general trends in the world, changes in the environment in which the business operates and particularly the expectations of the group served by the industry. Environmental analysis does not only identify

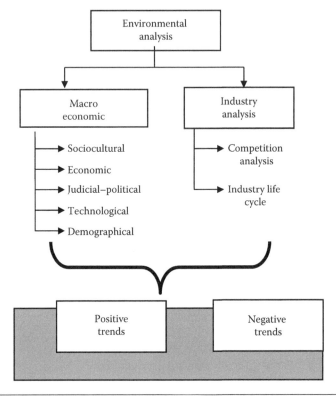

Figure 7.2   Environmental analysis.

current status, but also lays the basis for future forecasts or creation of
scenarios. As long as a business that is in interaction but cannot control many processes in the environment fails to follow up this change,
strategic planning would not make much sense.

Key considerations in environmental analysis are as follows:

- Current global status and development trends in the field of
  the business.
- Current domestic status and development trends in the field
  of the business.
- Critical issues that closely concern the business among the
  basic trends and problems in the world and in the country.
  How and in what direction these issues will affect the industry in which the business operates.
- Basic negativities and uncertainties faced by the business due
  to the conditions of the industry.

7.2.1 Macroeconomic Analysis

Macroeconomic variables are the variables that affect the businesses and their industry, not being under the control of businesses.

In order to benefit from the opportunities created by these variables and not to be caught unprepared, the businesses shall continuously follow their macroeconomic environments and act accordingly. Macroeconomic variables are illustrated in Figure 7.3:

- Demographical
- Economic
- Judicial–political
- Technological
- Sociocultural

The variables to be evaluated in order to compose changes and developments are specified as follows. This review should primarily be conducted at a global scale, and then at regional and country scales.

After collecting information about the present state, efforts must be made to identify trends in variables and future continuation of these trends. The purpose is to ascertain the impacts of variables in the macroeconomic environment on stakeholders.

Macroeconomic analysis presents the effects of developments on all the stakeholders of the business and assists to present the future picture of the industry more clearly.

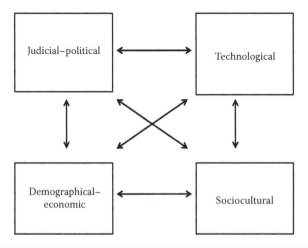

Figure 7.3 Macroeconomic analysis. (A novel management diagram.)

	DEMOGRAPHICAL	ECONOMIC	JUDICIAL–POLITICAL	TECHNOLOGICAL	SOCIOCULTURAL
Customers					
Government					
Financial Ins.					
Suppliers					
Shareholders					
Employees					
Result					

Figure 7.4 Macroeconomic analysis form. (Adapted from Porter, M.E., *Competitive Strategy: Techniques for Analyzing Industries and Competitors*, The Free Press, Florence, Italy, 1998.)

In order to analyze the effects of trends and developments within these variables on the industry, Figure 7.4 macroeconomic analysis form can be used. While composing this matrix

- On vertical axis—trends determined on variables
- On horizontal axis—stakeholders of business
- On elements of matrix—the anticipated effects of trends on the stakeholders should be input

The macroeconomic analysis form summarizes the status of the variables with respect to customers', government's, financial institutions', suppliers', shareholders', and employees' point of views. If macroeconomic factor will

- Turn into a better condition than now, then mark as +
- Remain unchanged, then mark as *blank*
- Turn into a worse condition than now, and then mark as –

Demographical variables:
Sociocultural and demographical variables may directly affect the living, working, producing, and consuming patterns and methods of societies. It is very important to analyze such variables from the perspectives of market and customers and evaluate their potential positive and negative impacts:

- Population growth rate
- Distribution of age
- Regional distribution of population
- Birth and mortality rates
- Literacy level

Economic variables:

Economic variables and elements may directly or indirectly affect market and industry structure, consumption patterns, and business structures. Therefore, they may directly affect the applicability and validity of various strategies:

- Change on gross national product
- Income distribution
- Interest rates
- Money supply
- Inflation rate
- Unemployment rate
- Exchange policy
- Savings

Judicial–political variables:

- Tax laws
- Competition laws
- Incentives
- Environmental laws
- Trade laws
- Political stability

Technological variables:

Changes and developments in product and production technology may affect the products/services produced by businesses, their suppliers, competitors, and customers. While technologic advancements may create new markets and new products, they may also have implications on costs and may totally change existing products and services:

- R&D expenses
- Innovation opportunity
- New products
- Technological change rate
- Rate of presentation of new products
- Efficiency increase by automation

Sociocultural variables:

- Change on lifestyles
- Career expectations

- Change on family structures
- Change on values and beliefs

7.2.2 Competition Analysis

Porter (1998) stated that, if a business is producing a product or service with a market, considerations like global and domestic market conditions, development/evolution trends of the demand for the subject product and/or service, price movements, changes in quality and standards, competition, etc., are laid down as a result of a comprehensive analysis of the powers in the industry.

The powers that affect a business at most are the groups that compose competition within the industry. The interaction among industry forces:

- Rivalry among existing companies
- Threat of potential new entrants
- Bargaining power of customers
- Threat of substitutes
- Bargaining power of suppliers
- Bargaining power of other stakeholders (government, trade unions, financial institutions, etc.)

The effects of these powers determine the strength of competition within the industry. In an industry where the power of these groups is high, the potential of profitability will be low. When one of these groups has a higher power, this would have negative implications for the industry, whereas a lower power would have positive implications. Figure 7.5 is a worksheet that can be used for competition analysis. Now, let us analyze these powers.

Industry definition:
The industry is defined as a group of businesses producing similar products or services.

- What is value-added chain in the industry?
- What are the inputs and outputs of each ring of the value-added chain?

	FIRMS IN THE INDUSTRY					THREATS OF NEW COMPANIES						COMPETITIVE POWER OF CUSTOMERS						COMPETITIVE POWER OF SUPPLIERS				
	Quantity of firms in the industry	Growth rate of the industry	Differences and the specialties of the products	Fixed costs	Cost to leave the industry	Costs of the companies in the industry related with the company size	Firms which have the customer-firm loyalty	The equity needed to enter the industry	Ability to reach channel of distribution	Cost advantage related with experience	Barriers to enter the industry	The share of the customer in the whole sale	Potential of production of the products by integration	Alternative suppliers	Cost of the change of the suppliers	Flexibility in the prices	The importance of the product for the customers	Quantity of firms in the industry and the production place	Unique products sale	Substitute goods in the market	Potential of production of the products by integration	The share of the sale of the supplier
Low																						
Avg.																						
High																						

Figure 7.5 Competition analysis form. (Redesigned from Porter, M.E., *Competitive Strategy: Techniques for Analyzing Industries and Competitors*, The Free Press, Florence, Italy, 1998.)

- What are the trends and developments giving direction to the industry in the world?
- What are the trends giving direction to the industry in country?
- Who are the clients?
- Under how many segments are clients gathered?
- What are the legal, political, economic, demographical, and technological changes?
- What are the strengths and weaknesses of the industry?
- What are the critical success indicators in the industry?
- In what direction is the industry moving?

- What is the annual turnover and growth rate of demand in the industry?
- How many businesses account for 80% of the industry's turnover?
- How does the industry evolve with technology?
- By what does demand vary?
- Are there companies leaving the industry?
- Have there been mergers in the industry recently?
- Are there alternative products to replace the existing products in the industry?
- Who are the clients of these alternative products?

Rivalry among existing companies:

- What are the factors that affect success and failure in the industry?
- Who are the leaders in the industry?
- Which businesses have the most advanced technology?
- Which businesses produce goods/services at lowest cost?
- Which customer segments do major businesses affect?
- What are the characteristics affecting the choice of businesses? (Compare price, service, etc.)
- Which businesses receive customer loyalty?
- What are the turnover, growth rate, profitability rate, market share, net profit of major businesses?
- What are the resources used by major businesses (facility, building, capital)?
- How many businesses account for 80% of industry turnover?
- Is there a cartel in the industry?
- What are the supply capacity, turnover, size, and growth rate of the industry?
- Is product imported? What is its price and quality?
- What are the market shares of products?
- How would you classify products in terms of product life cycle?
- How is product differentiation in the industry? Does this differentiation reflect onto product price?
- What are the fixed and variable cost rates of businesses in the industry?

- What is the impact of fixed costs on prices?
- What is the capacity utilization rate in the industry?
- What is the impact of capacity utilization rate on prices?
- What are the costs of exit from the industry?
- Are there businesses leaving the industry?
- Have there been mergers in the industry recently?

Competition in an industry is high if

- The number of active businesses are high
- The growth rate of the industry decelerates or accelerates rapidly
- The characteristics of products/ services are not very different
- The fixed costs are high
- Cost of leaving industry is high

Threat of potential new entrants:

- Which are the new entrants in the industry? How are the shareholder structures of these businesses?
- What are the turnover and growth rates of new entrants in the industry?
- How much investment capital is necessary for entering the industry?
- Are there multinational businesses that have entered, or are planning to enter, the industry?
- Is there a *learning curve* impact?
- Are there factors that pose difficulties for new entrants to enter the industry, such as copyrighted products, dominance over distribution channels, qualification certificates, etc.?
- Are there government restrictions for entrance to the industry?
- What are entrance restrictions?
- How many businesses account for 80% of industry turnover?
- Which businesses receive customer loyalty?
- How does the industry evolve with technology?
- What are the trends, opportunities, restrictions, and investments in the industry?
- Costs of exit from the industry?

The possibility of new entrants to threat the existing businesses within the industry depends on the level of entry barriers.

Entry barriers are high at the rate

- Of having low costs due to the size of the companies within the industry
- Of having brands within the industry
- Of having high investment requirement
- Of accessibility to distribution channels being hard
- Of having high learning curve effect
- Of having various limitations by the government for the new entrants

Bargaining power of customers:

- Who are customers?
- Who are not customers?
- Under how many segments are customers grouped?
- What are the first five expectations of customers in order of importance?
- To what extent can these expectations be met?
- In what areas do customers operate?
- What are the characteristics that make the customers important and privileged?
- What are the critical success factors in the industry?
- What are the reasons for customer complaints?
- How is the geographical distribution of customers?
- How are the income/education/age/status of customers?
- Who influence customers most when they take purchase decisions?
- By what does demand vary?
- What is the cost of changing seller for customers?
- Are there any customers starting production in the industry, or is there such a tendency?
- By what distribution channels are customers reached? Their accessibility?

Customer is powerful if

- It purchases in large quantities of the products/services of the supplier
- It has the potential of producing products/services by vertical integration

- There are alternative suppliers
- The cost of changing supplier is not high
- It is sensitive to price and service variations
- The purchased product/service does not bear an importance for its production/operation

Threat of substitutes:

- Are there substitutes that can replace existing products in the industry?
- How is the development trend of substitutes in the industry?
- Who are the customers of these substitutes?
- What is the cost of product replacement for customers?
- What are the impacts of substitute products' prices?

Substitutes are products/services that cover the same requirements in different ways. In industries where substitutes are plenty and the customers have low product-changing costs, companies can face with less profit.

Bargaining power of suppliers:

- Who are suppliers?
- Who are not suppliers?
- How many businesses account for 80% of turnover?
- What are the raw material sources, characteristics and costs?
- Are suppliers eager for vertical integration?
- Has any supplier purchased a business in the industry?
- Are there any partnerships or coalitions between suppliers and businesses in the industry?
- What is the share of products purchased from suppliers in production cost?
- What is the importance of businesses in the industry for the supplier?
- To what extent can suppliers meet expectations?
- What are the most important complaints about suppliers?
- Does replacement of supplier pose a difficulty?
- How is the communication with suppliers?
- What is the rate of purchases from domestic markets to imports?
- From which countries are products imported?
- What sort of a policy pursued regarding the development of suppliers?

Suppliers are powerful if

- The industry is composed of limited suppliers
- Their products/services are unique and exclusive
- There is no substitutes in the market
- They have the potential to compete with the current customers through vertical integration
- The purchases compose a small portion of their income

Bargaining power of other stakeholders:

Other stakeholders are government, financial institutions, trade unions, etc., that have impacts on competition. The effects of these groups on competition shall be included in the analysis.

Competitive forces—"Manufacturing Business X":

COMPETITION OF EXISTING BUSINESSES	ABS	CBS	
Number of existing firms	<15	<10	
Industry growth rate (%)	10	10	
Product characteristics difference	No	No	
Service	Yes	Yes	
Fixed costs	5	3	Costs evaluated on a scale of 5
Industry exit cost ($)	<6 M	<1 M	

For ABS, level of competition is high despite the low number of businesses operating in the industry due to other factors. For CBS, although competition among businesses is expected to be low, it is high because of the price pressure created by traditional plaster.

THREATS OF NEW BUSINESSES	ABS	CBS	
Number of big firms	11	4	
Brand recognition	No	No	
Entry cost ($)	<6 M	<2 M	
Difficulty of reaching distribution channels	4	4	Degree of difficulty evaluated on a scale of 5
Cost advantages	5	4	Degree of advantage evaluated on a scale of 5
Government barriers	4	1	Degree of difficulty evaluated on a scale of 5

For ABS, the possibility of new players to threaten existing businesses in the industry is low, considering the previous table. For CBS, although the possibility of new players to threaten existing businesses in the industry seems to be high, new entrants would expand the market since industrial plaster has a lower market share relative to traditional plaster.

POWER OF CUSTOMERS	ABS	CBS	
Demand power of customer	5	5	Demand evaluated on a scale of 5
Backward integration potential	1	3	Production potential evaluated on a scale of 5
Alternative sellers	Yes	Yes	
Brand switching cost	1	1	
Sensitivity on price and service change	5	5	
Satisfaction w.r.t existing products	5	5	

Considering the previous table, customers are strong for all product groups.

POWER OF SUPPLIERS	ABS	CBS
Number of firms in industry	<15	<10
Number of suppliers:		
Gypsum and cement	<15	<20
Chemical a	5	5
Chemical b	<10	<10
Packaging	1	6
Forward integration capability	1	1

For ABS, gypsum suppliers are not strong in the light of the previous table. For CBS, cement suppliers are strong despite the previous table. Chemical suppliers are strong in this product group since they are all multinational manufacturers. Packaging products are monopolistic for ABS. None of these suppliers has a structure suitable for advanced integration.

THREAT OF SUBSTITUTE PRODUCTS	ABS	CBS
	Plaster board, cement-based plaster	All exterior facade cladding, gypsum, black cement plaster

Using the five competitive forces:

The results of analyses conducted in the light of these and similar considerations will be given in the summary (Porter 1998):

- Each force needs to be evaluated in terms of—does it make the market attractiveness
  - High?
  - Moderate?
  - Low?
- Each force needs to be evaluated in terms of its relative importance.

Figure 7.6 shows an example of evaluating the competitive forces. You need to look at the competitive forces not in isolation but in terms of how they interact with one another. For instance, buyers may seek to enter the market (via backward integration). Or suppliers may also seek entry (via forward integration). Equally, buyers may look wider for

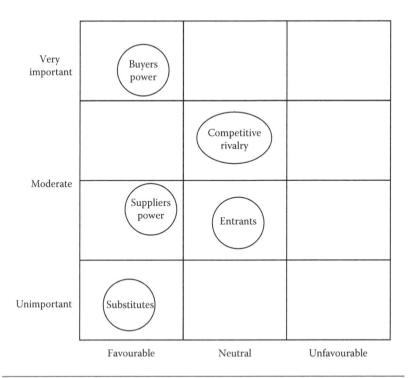

Figure 7.6 Evaluation of the competitive forces—*example.* (Redesigned from Porter, M.E., *Competitive Strategy: Techniques for Analyzing Industries and Competitors*, The Free Press, Florence, Italy, 1998.)

sources of supply (if competitive rivalry is low), enticing new entrants in. Finally, new substitutes might be sought where buyer power is low.

When the industry changes significantly, it is frequently not because of one competitive force, but because of changes of two or possibly three forces combining together.

Where firms apply the five competitive forces, they frequently ignore or fail to deal systematically with the relative importance of each force. Figure 7.6 helps to avoid this problem by separating out "unfavorable" ratings of the five forces against their relative importance. This relative importance will differ between industries and particular markets.

Figure 7.7 shows an example of competitive forces status. In the example, taking the five forces as a whole, it can be seen that the industry is currently relatively favorable to making a good and longer-term profit.

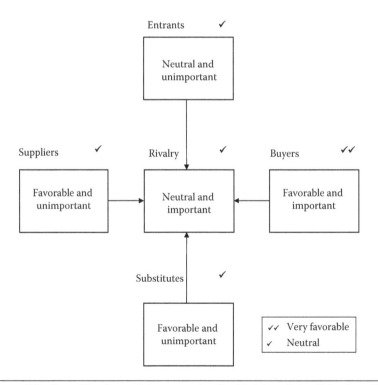

Figure 7.7 Competitive forces status—example. (Reprinted from Porter, M.E., *Competitive Strategy: Techniques for Analyzing Industries and Competitors*, The Free Press, Florence, Italy, 1998.)

7.2.3 Industry Life Cycle

Vernon (1979) stated that each industry passes through the phases of introductory, growth, maturity, and finally declining. The phase that the industry is within facilitates the estimation of impacts and trends of powers defined in competition analysis. Figure 7.8 shows the industry life cycle.

If the product/service presented in a new industry covers a special requirement, the individuals will buy without considering its price.

Competition increases by the new entrants to the industry and thus the price starts to decrease. Businesses try to decrease their costs more than their competitors due to their experiences and sizes or try to avoid price competition by differentiating their products.

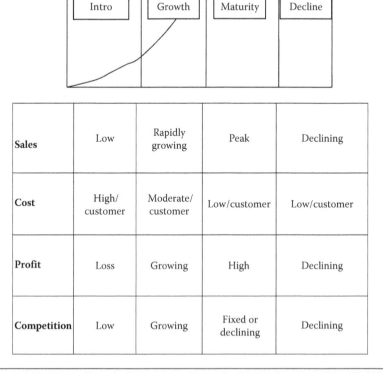

	Intro	Growth	Maturity	Decline
Sales	Low	Rapidly growing	Peak	Declining
Cost	High/ customer	Moderate/ customer	Low/customer	Low/customer
Profit	Loss	Growing	High	Declining
Competition	Low	Growing	Fixed or declining	Declining

Figure 7.8   Industry life cycle. (Reprinted from Vernon, R., *Oxf. Bull. Econ. Stat.*, 41(4), 255, 1979.)

When the industry reaches the maturity phase, the customers have better information on the products/services and when the products/services meet the minimum expectations price composes the most important purchasing criteria.

During the declining phase, the growth rates on the sales of product and/or service decreases, the businesses try to use their plans for alternative opportunities or try to sell them. By the mergers within the industry, a few but strong competitors remain. These companies should create new markets or enter into international markets.

IDENTIFY COMPETITIVE ADVANTAGES

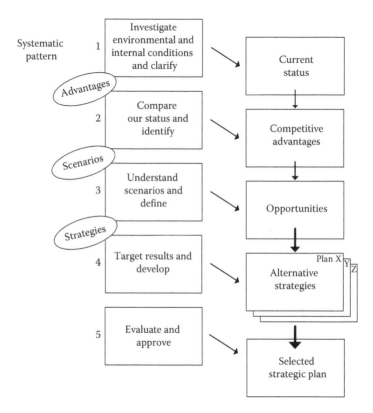

Now is the time to compare the business' status with meaningful standards to determine which value factors are competitive advantages and more. Competitive analysis must evaluate a limited number of strengths and weaknesses relative to the opportunities targeted in the business' current and future competitive environment, and identify the competitive advantages of the business.

A factor is considered a competitive advantage if it is something the business does (or has in the future the capacity to do) particularly well relative to the abilities of existing or potential competitors. A firm gains competitive advantage by performing these strategically important factors for cheaper or better than its competitors. A competitive advantage is present if the business consistently offers the customer something that is *different* to what competitors are offering, and that difference represents something *valuable* for the customer.

A factor is considered a weakness if it is something the firm does poorly or does not have the capacity to do, whereas key rivals have the capacity.

How should the key internal factors be evaluated and valued as competitive advantages or weaknesses? Sources of meaningful standards used to evaluate internal factors, categorized by strengths and weaknesses, are discussed in this section. There are three basic perspectives:

- Stage of market evolution
- Comparison with competitors
- Comparison with key success factors in the business' industry

Identifying competitive factors requires an external focus. When key internal factors through analysis of the past and present performance are isolated, the next step is to identify industry conditions/trends and compare with competitors. Changing industry conditions can lead to the need to reexamine internal strengths and weaknesses in light of newly emerging determinants of success in the industry (Pearce and Robinson 2011).

To develop or revise a strategy, a business would identify the few factors on which success will most likely depend. Businesses are looking for *the competitive factors* that appear most critical for success can vary even among them within the same industry.

Figure 8.1 summarizes the development of a business profile. Pearce and Robinson (2011) stated that, in step one, key aspects of the business's operation to the firm's strategic direction called *strategic internal factors* are audited and examined. Then evaluate the business' status on these factors by comparing their current condition with past abilities of the business.

The second step is very critical. Businesses seek some comparative basis—linked to key industry or product/market conditions—against which to determine more accurately whether the business' condition

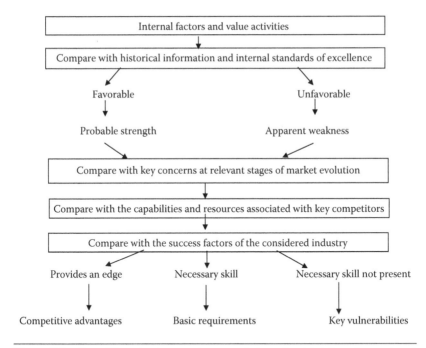

Figure 8.1   Competitive advantages and success factors. (Reprinted from Pearce, J. and Robinson, R. *Strategic Management: Formulation, Implementation and Control*, McGraw-Hill Higher Education, Columbus, OH, 2011.)

on a particular factor represents potential competitive advantages or weaknesses. As it is said, businesses use three perspectives to do this: (1) Requirements for success across different product/market stages of evolution, (2) what competitors are capable of doing, and (3) perceived key requirements for success in which they compete. The result of the second step should be a determination of whether key internal factors are as follows:

1. *Competitive advantages*: Factors providing the business with an edge compared to its competitors, and therefore key factors around which to build the business' strategy.
2. *Basic business requirements*: Factors that are important capabilities for the business to have but are also typical of every viable competitor—does not represent a potential source of any strategic advantage.
3. *Key vulnerabilities*: Factors on which the business currently lacks the necessary skill, knowledge, or resources to compete effectively. This assessment is also a key input because

businesses will want to avoid choosing strategies that depend on factors in this category. And businesses usually target key vulnerabilities as areas for special attention so as to remediate and change this situation.

Table 8.1 is a worksheet that is used for determination of competitive advantages and so through comparison. The next step in competitive analysis is to provide the results, or business profile, as input into the systematic strategic planning process. This input is vital during the opportunity determination section. Remember that each section in the process often overlaps another section.

8.1 Comparison with Basic Factors of Industry Life Cycle

The requirements for success in market segments evolve and change over time for identifying and evaluating the business' strengths and weaknesses. Four general stages of market evolution is shown in Figure 7.7.

The early development of a market, for example, entails minimal growth in sales, major R&D emphasis, rapid technological change in the product, operating losses, and a need for sufficient resources or slack to support a temporarily unprofitable operation. Success at this stage may be associated with technical skill with being first in new markets or with having a marketing advantage that creates widespread awareness. Table 8.2 summarizes the necessary strengths in start-up stage.

The strengths necessary for success change in the growth stage. Rapid growth brings new competitors into the market. Such factors as brand recognition, product/market differentiation, and the financial resources to support both heavy marketing expenses and the effect of price competition on cash flow can be key strengths at this stage. Table 8.3 summarizes the necessary strengths in growth stage.

In the maturity stage, market growth continues but at a decreasing rate. The number of market segments begins to expand, while technological change in product design slows considerably. The result is usually more intense in competition and promotional or pricing advantages or differentiation become the key internal strengths. Technological change in process design becomes intense as many

Table 8.1 Comparison with Main Competitors and Industry Average

	FACTORS	OUR BUSINESS	MAIN COMPETITOR(S)	INDUSTRY
Marketing	Firm's products/services; breadth of product line			
	Concentration of sales in a few products or to a few customers			
	Ability to gather needed information about markets			
	Market share or submarket shares			
	Product/service mix and expansion potential			
	Channels of distribution: number, coverage, and control			
	Effective sales organization			
	Product/service image, reputation, and quality			
	Imaginative, efficient, and effective sales promotion and advertising			
	Pricing strategy and pricing flexibility			
	Procedures for digesting market feedback and developing new products, services, or markets			
	After-sale service and follow-up			
	Goodwill/brand loyalty			
Finance and Accounting	Ability to raise short-term capital			
	Ability to raise long-term capital: debt/equity			
	Corporate-level resources			
	Cost of capital relative to industry and competitors			
	Tax considerations			
	Relations with owners, investors and stockholders			
	Leverage positions			
	Cost of entry and barriers to entry			

(*Continued*)

Table 8.1 (*Continued*)   Comparison with Main Competitors and Industry Average

FACTORS	OUR BUSINESS	MAIN COMPETITOR(S)	INDUSTRY
Price–earnings ratio			
Working capital; flexibility of capital structure			
Effective cost control, ability to reduce costs			
Financial size			
Efficient and effective accounting system for cost, budget, and profit planning			

	FACTORS	OUR BUSINESS	MAIN COMPETITOR(S)	INDUSTRY
Production/ Technical	Raw materials cost and availability			
	Inventory control systems; inventory turnover			
	Location of facilities; layout and utilization			
	Economies of scale			
	Technical efficiency of facilities and utilization of capacity			
	Effective use of subcontracting			
	Degree of vertical integration, value added and profit margin			
	Efficiency and cost/benefit of equipment			
	Effective operation control procedures			
	Cost and technological competencies relative to industry and competitors			
	Research and development/ technology/innovation			
	Patents, trademarks and similar			
Personnel	Management personnel			
	Employees' skill and morale			
	Labor relations compared to industry and competition			
	Efficient and effective personnel policies			

(*Continued*)

Table 8.1 (*Continued*) Comparison with Main Competitors and Industry Average

FACTORS	OUR BUSINESS	MAIN COMPETITOR(S)	INDUSTRY
Effective use of incentives to motivate performance			
Ability to level peaks and valleys of employment			
Employee turnover and absenteeism			
Specialized skills			
Experience			
Organization and Management Organizational structure			
Firm's image and prestige			
Firm's record for achieving objectives			
Organization of communication system			
Overall organizational control system			
Organizational climate, culture			
Use of systematic procedures and techniques			
Top-management skill, capacities, and interest			
Strategic planning system			
Intra organizational synergy			

Table 8.2 Start-Up Stage

Financial	Revenue is growing
	Profit is nonexistent
	Cash flow is negative
Marketplace	Getting product to market
	Building market share
	High level of customer intimacy
Supply chain	Searching for resources
	Looking for partners
	Changing rapidly
Operations	Simple, informal structure
	Few policies, procedures, and processes
	Emerging information systems
	Focus is on survival

Table 8.3 Growth Stage

Financial	Revenue is growing even more rapidly
	Moving past break-even
	Cash flow is negative but improving
Marketplace	Coping with a volume of opportunities
	Expanding channels of distribution
	Managing customer expectations
Supply chain	Becoming stable
	Increasing buyer power
	Examining business partnerships
Operations	Organizational structure is not keeping pace
	Emergence of policies, procedures, and processes
	Information systems are struggling to keep up
	Focus on maximizing production

competitors seek to provide the product in the most efficient manner. Where R&D was critical in the development stage, efficient production has now become crucial to a business's continued success in the broader market segments. Table 8.4 summarizes the necessary strengths in maturity stage.

In saturation/decline stage, strengths and weaknesses center on cost advantages, superior supplier or customer relationships, and financial control. Table 8.5 summarizes the necessary strengths in decline stage. The relative importance of various determinants of success differs across stages of market evolution.

Table 8.4 Maturity Stage

Financial	Revenue growth rate slows
	Profits are strong
	Cash flow is positive
Marketplace	Building product line extensions
	Creating value added services
	Renewed focus on the customer
Supply chain	Negotiate long-term contracts
	Leveraging buyer power
	Expanding "supplier" linkages
Operations	Organization structure has become complex
	Policies, procedures, and processes abound
	Information systems focus on control
	Focus is on maximizing efficiency and operational excellence

Table 8.5 Decline Stage

Financial	Revenue is flat or declining
	Profits are flat
	Cash flow is positive
	Little or no reinvestment
Marketplace	Declining market share
	Losing customers to alternative solutions
Supply chain	Price is the only issue
	Value added partnerships dissolve
Operations	Organization shrinks
	Information systems are in maintenance mode
	Focus is on survival

8.2 Comparison with Main Competitors

A major focus in determining a business' competitive power and weaknesses is its comparison with existing (and potential) competitors. Table 8.1 is a worksheet that can be used for identifying competitive advantages and success factors. Businesses in the same industry often have different marketing skills, financial resources, operating facilities and locations, technical know-how, brand image, levels of integration, managerial talent, etc. These different internal capabilities can become relative strengths (or weaknesses) depending on the strategy the business chooses. A business should compare capabilities with those of its rivals, thereby isolating key strengths and weaknesses.

8.2.1 Strategies and Objectives of Competitors

The most important competitors of a business are the ones that present products/services to the same target audience with a similar strategy. (This group of companies is called strategic group.)

Determination of the strategic groups will provide a more accurate definition of competition. The businesses within the same strategic group are more similar than other businesses within the industry, and thus the competition among them is stronger.

The business should have as much information as possible regarding marketing, production, R&D, financial and human resources strategies, product qualities, distribution channels, etc., of their competitors.

After determining the competitors' strategies, objectives, and growth or merging plans, market share, profitability, technological leadership, service leadership, etc., of the competitors should also be investigated.

8.2.2 Strengths and Weaknesses of Competitors

The ability of competitors to apply their strategies and reach their objectives depends on their sources and abilities. In order to define the strengths and weaknesses of competitors, the business shall reach out to some competitors and assemble information regarding their new investments and also their assumptions.

The information can be obtained from secondary sources, personal experiences, conversations, and also can be composed by the market researches where the customers and suppliers are included.

8.2.3 Strategic Approaches of Competitors

Generally the companies within an industry can be grouped under four categories with respect to their strategic characteristics.

- *Defenders*: These companies try to decrease their costs by making their operations more efficient and try to defend their positions in the market.
- *Entrepreneurs*: These are companies that continuously create new products/services and new market opportunities.
- *Analyzers*: These are companies that act sometimes like defenders and sometimes like entrepreneurs.
- *Followers*: These are companies that do not have a specific strategy and act according to the environmental pressures.

Predicting competitor moves—some clues:

- Patterns in currently visible, tactical behavior
- Competitor's mission or vision statements or of strategic intent
- Published accounts and annual reports
- Knowledge of their competitive recipes and paradigm (how they operate and think)
- Change in leadership or ownership
- Potential investment plans
- Financial resources—evaluating their war chest

The key aspects of how a business/business area competes are listed at the left *competitive criteria*. The criteria need to be those most important in competing (e.g., customer value—most important to the customer).

8.3 Comparison with Industry Success Factors*

The key determinants of success in an industry may be used to identify the internal competitive power and weaknesses of a business. Use of industry average to evaluate a business' capacity for success has become a popular technique. Sources of success factors are as follows:

1. The *architecture* of the business, that is, its internal structure
2. The *reputation* of the business, that is, the way key stakeholders view it
3. The way the business *innovates*, that is, its ability to come up with valuable ideas
4. The business's *strategic assets*, that is, valuable assets to which it has access

They can be related to four specific sources of success determinants: *costs*, *knowledge*, *relationships*, and *structure*.

8.3.1 Cost Sources

- *Lower input costs*: This can include raw materials, energy, or labor. Lower input costs can be gained by a number of means. Particularly important are access to unique sources of inputs and achieving buying power over suppliers.
- *Economies of scale*: Unit costs tend to fall as output increases. Fixed costs are those that must be valid regardless of the output achieved. These typically include head office costs, marketing, sales, and development activity. A larger output means that these costs are being used more productively.
- *Experience curve economies*: Economies of scale depend on output in a particular period, experience curve economies are a result of *cumulative output*. Experience curve economies may be sought in other parts of the business' value addition process such as sales, marketing, procurement, etc.

---

* This section is adapted from Wickham (2004).

- *Technological innovation*: A technological innovation can provide a cost advantage by enabling value to be added more efficiently. Such innovation often relates to production technology, but in principle it can apply to any value adding activity within the organization.

8.3.2 Knowledge Sources

- *Product knowledge*: It must be used to create offerings that are more attractive to buyers. Product knowledge must be used in conjunction with knowledge of the market buyers.
- *Market knowledge*: Market knowledge insights into the way the market functions such as the needs of the customer, the way in which customers buy, and what can be used to influence them.
- *Technical knowledge*: It must be used to offer the customer something different: a better product, a lower cost product, or a better service. Product and technical knowledge arise from research and development activities. Market knowledge comes from market research and market analysis.

8.3.3 Relationship Sources

- *Relationship with customers*: Much depends on the nature of the products being sold to the customer and the number of customers the business has to deal with. Relationships can be personal, that are created through individual contact. The sales–buyer interaction is both a one-to-one contact and through which value can flow from the business to its customers. If a personal contact is not possible, then contact may be sustained via the media through advertising and public relations.
- *Relationship with suppliers*: Suppliers are best regarded as partners in the development of an end-market if its suppliers themselves show flexibility and responsiveness. Further, suppliers can be encouraged to innovate on behalf of the business. A customer working with its suppliers can address the end-market better and create more overall value.
- *Relationship with investors*: They respond not only to actual returns but also if they feel their interests are being properly

addressed. When things are not going too well, the support of investors is invaluable. The support of investors can be maintained by developing a strategy to communicate actively with them. This will involve managing the investors' expectations, building their confidence in the venture, and avoiding surprises that lead investors to make hasty judgments.

- *Relationship with employees*: Understanding the employees' motivations and adopting the right leadership strategies.

8.3.4 Structural Sources

Structural advantages arise as a consequence not so much of what the business does but the way it goes about doing things. This is a function not only of its formal structure, the predefined way in which individuals will relate to each other but also in its informal structure, the unofficial web of relationships and communication links that actually define it and its culture that governs how those relationships will function and evolve.

This should be more responsive to the needs of customers and so be quicker to offer them new products and services.

Another structural advantage can arise if the individuals who make it up emphasize tasks (what needs to be done) rather than roles (what they feel their job descriptions say they should do). Such an attitude enables the business to be flexible, to focus on its customers, and keep fixed costs to a minimum.

8.4 Competitive Advantages, Success Factors, and Weaknesses

If a business is to enjoy a competitive advantage over a long time it must be one that competitors find expensive to copy. What will be offered to the marketplace that is unique and valuable is the competitive advantage. In short, Pearce and Robinson (2011) say the following:

1. *Competitive advantages*: Factors providing the business with an edge compared to its competitors, and therefore become key factors around which one should build the business' strategy.

Table 8.6   Competitive Advantages and Success Factors—Manufacturing Business X

	FACTORS	COMPETITIVE ADVANTAGES	SUCCESS FACTORS
Organization/ General Management	1. Flexible and horizontal relations facilitate decision making	☑	
	2. Participatory and sharing management	☑	
	3. Broad investment vision		☑
	4. Prestigious company name		☑
	5. Experienced management staff undertaking responsibilities		☑
	6. Strategic planning and budget discipline		☑
Personnel	1. Competent, experienced and responsible staff	☑	
	2. Qualified and young labor force	☑	
	3. Specialized staff		☑
Production/Technical	1. Ease of raw material supply, except for gypsum	☑	
	2. Good supplier relations		☑
	3. Registered trademarks		
	4. Effective use of subcontractors	☑	
	5. Cost advantage through extraction of sand from own sandpit	☑	
	6. Production control procedures		
	7. Effective quality control		☑
	8. Vertical integration	☑	
	9. Technical team competence		☑
	10. Product development capacity		☑
	11. Development potential of products	☑	
Marketing	1. Product diversity	☑	
	2. Market leader in manufacturing of ready-made gypsum products	☑	
	3. Presales application service		☑
	4. Qualification and competence in ABS and ÇBS distribution channels		☑
	5. Quality and branded products and ABS and ÇBS products	☑	
	6. Technical support department		☑
	7. Strong references		☑
Finance/Accounting	1. Automation and integration through system investments, resulting in effective accounting, costing, and budgeting	☑	
	2. Effective cost control		☑
	3. High credibility		☑

(*Continued*)

Table 8.6 (*Continued*)   Competitive Advantages and Success Factors—Manufacturing Business X

FACTORS	COMPETITIVE ADVANTAGES	SUCCESS FACTORS
4. Positive communication with shareholders, strong shareholder structure	☑	
5. High equity profitability	☑	
6. High working capital ratio	☑	
7. High profit margin	☑	
8. Long-term capital raising capacity		☑
9. Image of a tax-paying and strong company	☑	

2. *Basic success factors*: Factors that are important capabilities for the business to have but are also typical of every viable competitor—does not represent a potential source of any strategic advantage.

3. *Key vulnerabilities*: Factors on which the business currently lacks the necessary skill, knowledge, or resources to compete effectively. This assessment is also a key input because firms will want to avoid choosing strategies that depend on factors in this category. And businesses usually target key vulnerabilities as areas for special attention so as to remediate and change this situation.

(Table 8.6 is a worksheet that can be used for listing competitive advantages and success factors.) As a result of this section, the answers of the following questions will be given:

- Who are we?
- What do we do?
- What is our profession?
- Who aren't we?
- What can't we do?
- What is not our business?

9

UNDERSTAND SCENARIOS AND DEFINE OPPORTUNITIES

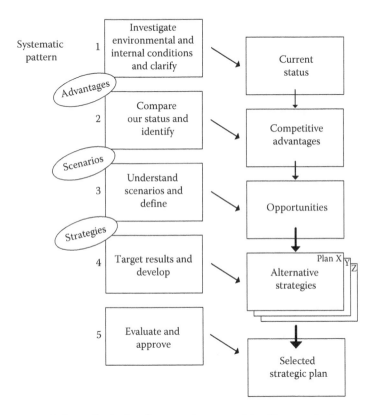

It is intended to find the factors that would affect and change the outlook mostly in the current status and anticipated future, based on the results obtained from environmental analysis. The external variables that are most sensitive and that would affect the results most if changed are identified and value impact matrix are created.

In short, using the trends to be revealed by the environmental analysis, it is possible to anticipate how the field of business in which we operate or plan to enter will evolve in the future. (It must be remembered that an external variable with ignorable impact in current status may have an unexpectedly increased influence in the future depending on other factors, which could lead to changes in the results of all analyses conducted.) For instance, information may be obtained about the way how customer needs and expectations will evolve and develop in the future.

Assumptions are made on these variables, for instance, through the brainstorming approach. The status is reviewed according to the assumptions and the results to be obtained are evaluated. It is important that this step is continuously repeated taking into consideration evolving conditions and innovations. Thus, assumptions are grouped under various scenarios, their potential positive and negative impacts on the industry are identified, and the potential status in the industry is defined. Scenarios:

- Internally consistent views of the future.
- Focus on discontinuity and change.
- Explore the impact of the change on key players and how they respond to the environment.

In conclusion, taking into consideration the characteristics of the business that offer competitive advantages, the potential opportunities for the business in the industry are identified. Figure 9.1 shows the procedure of identifying opportunities.

9.1 Assumptions on Future

Assumptions are critical in formulating a successful strategy. In other words, the success of strategic plans depends largely on the actualization of assumptions made during the planning process.

Assumptions imply the external factors that are not under the direct control of the business preparing the strategic plan but that can affect the progress and success of the strategic plan. After reviewing sociocultural factors, technological factors, political environmental, legal conditions, macroeconomic factors and variables originating from international systems in the environmental analysis, the tendencies of related parties such as competitors, customers, and suppliers must reflect onto the systematic of strategic planning as assumptions.

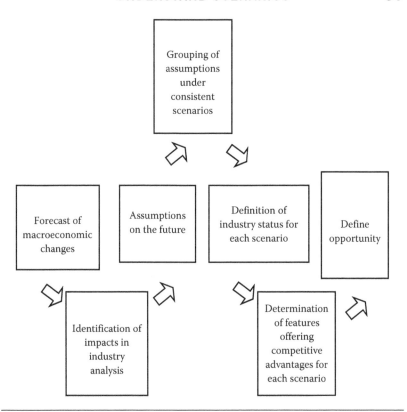

Figure 9.1 Procedure of identifying opportunities.

First, key external variables are identified. Assumptions are made for the values of quantitative and qualitative variables (through brainstorming or statistical models). Brainstorming and/or statistical models are popular estimation techniques:

- Brainstorming is a nonnumerical estimation technique. While conducting scenario analysis, instruments like participatory meetings bringing together various groups concerning the business are used. For the efforts to be made in this scope, it is possible to outsource specialized services, such as the use of facilitators (moderators) who will neutrally facilitate participatory meetings.
- Statistical models are numerical techniques including relations and other econometric models. However, it is based on historical data, and error margin increases as the structure of relations changes in time.

Make your assumptions as specific as possible—set parameters (e.g., is project x will be running smoothly for users by December y). The most significant estimation errors arise from wrong assumptions, adaptations of reflecting today's trends to future.

For a successful strategic planning, it is necessary that the assumptions are discussed and matured by the strategic planning team. This is because assumptions will represent a common base for individual units throughout all phases and sections of strategic planning. Therefore, the same assumptions must be used across all departments.

9.1.1 Forecasting the Quantitative Impacts of Macroeconomic Variables

The value of utilizing such a multidimensional analysis of the future environment lies in the fact that

- It makes explicit all the environmental assumptions on which planning should be based.
- It integrates the *social* factors and the *business* factors into the planning framework.
- It identifies the spectrum of probable future constraints and opportunities for business performance.
- It provides an opportunity for determining needed business responses to changing conditions.

Essentially, the forecasting is done in four steps:

1. Select critical indicators:
   - Identify the industry's key indicators (trends).
   - Undertake literature search to identify potential future events impacting the key trends.
2. Establish past behavior for each indicator:
   - Establish the historical performance for each indicator.
   - Use data for the trend impact analysis.
   - Analyze reasons for past behavior of each trend:
     - Demographic and social
     - Economic
     - Political and legislative
     - Technological

3. Verify potential future events:
   - Interrogate Delphi panel:
     – Evaluate past trends.
     – Assess the potential impact of future events.
     – Assess the probability of future events.
     – Forecast future values.
   - Specify and document assumptions.
   - Specify and document rationale for projected values.
4. Forecast each indicator:
   - Operate the trend impact and cross impact analysis to establish the range of future values.
   - Analyze forecast results.

An example of using regression model for forecasting the quantitative impacts of macroeconomic variables:

"As far as the dynamics of construction industry and construction materials subsector are concerned, the primary factors affecting supply and demand growth in the industry are

- GNP growth rate
- Growth in number of households
- Population growth rate
- Growth in number of licensed buildings
- Increase in unit m^2 price of buildings

Therefore, the following example involves the projection of these five rates, taking as a basis the past 20 years. Forecasts were obtained to be taken as the denominator of each rate. These reveal the forecasts of trends for future rates as well as the number of licensed apartments that forms the numerator in each rate. Often, an arithmetic mean of these rates may be used.

$$y = -411.7 + 0.1117x_1 + 1.526x_2 + 0.1236x_3 + 1.8409x_4 + 0.3820x_5$$

where
x_1 is the growth of GNP per capita
x_2 is the growth in number of households
x_3 is the population growth
x_4 is the growth in number of licensed buildings
x_5 is the increase in unit m^2 building prices"

YEARS	LICENSED NO. OF FLATS GROWTH (000) (y)	GNP PER CAPITA INCREASE (000) (x_1)	GROWTH HOUSE HOLDS (x_2)	POP. GROWTH RATE (x_3)	LICENSED BUILD. GROWTH (x_4)	BUILDING M2 PRICE INCREASE (x_5)
1977	216	11	295	853	25	6
1978	237	−11	307	872	26	44
1979	252	−31	323	890	31	33
1980	204	−57	330	908	32	−49
1981	144	26	229	1102	27	−19
1982	160	6	235	1148	49	−7
1983	169	20	242	1176	37	−3
1984	189	53	247	1206	38	−6
1985	259	22	255	1236	77	13
1986	393	56	276	1127	143	17
1987	498	99	283	1128	160	−1
1988	474	−10	292	1154	168	7
1989	413	−8	300	1178	132	19
1990	381	96	308	1205	71	30
1991	393	−24	317	1228	77	21
1992	473	66	326	1258	123	7
1993	548	95	335	1285	136	5
1994	524	−128	345	1314	132	−46
1995	508	92	355	1343	99	15
1996	446	91	364	1372	94	−1

9.1.2 Analysis of Competitive Forces Impacts

Intensifying *rivalry* may either squeeze suppliers' prices or may encourage closer collaboration via partnerships.

Substitutes might take existing suppliers out of play. This underlines the importance of thinking about substitutes both within your own part of the industry chain, but also either up or down the chain.

Buyer power might intensify rivalry through buyers increasing the extent to which they shop around. Also, buyers might be tempted into developing upstream in the industry chain by entry.

Here, the overall demand/supply balance is a very important factor in adding to, or subtracting from, the negotiating power of *suppliers.*

9.2 Grouping of Assumptions as Scenarios

As a result of studies and researches to be conducted for assumptions, the business will group the scenarios for its own industry, and summarize them in a table.

Against the developments that may occur in the environment beyond the control of the business, the business will prepare alternative scenarios for the future. Based on the assumption that any unexpected development may occur in the future, the business must always be prepared for such cases and constantly follow up the developments. As a natural consequence of this approach, scenarios need to be based on a flexible structure and revised continuously according to trends and developments.

The purpose of scenario analysis is to make decisions for the future based on a limited number of scenarios produced. Various views and expectations will arise while developing scenarios. The scenarios produced must encompass these views to the extent possible. Points to consider while developing scenarios:

- What will be the boundaries of the industry 5 years later? What are the current boundaries and the value-added chains linked to the industry that you consider joining?
- Which actors may significantly affect the development of scenarios?
- Who, and to what extent, will be affected from the developments in the industry?
- What are the factors giving direction to the future of the industry? What are the critical unknown factors, rather than the possible factors to forecast?
- What is the most important change that will occur in the sector's structure and balance of powers?
- While scenarios are written in detail, they must be freed from internal inconsistencies.

- Detailed scenarios should not describe the situation 5 years later, but rather tell about the developments that would take us there in 5 years.

9.2.1 Grouping of Assumptions

Position the key assumptions which underpin an issue. Write the assumption in shorthand on a yellow post-it and position it relative to others on the grid. Test out relative and absolute positioning. Figure 9.2 can be used as a certainty and importance worksheet.

9.2.2 Generating Scenarios

Generate scenarios by testing out judgments and identifying interdependencies as is shown in Figure 9.3:

1. Prepare a list of basic assumptions using Figure 9.2.
2. Rank the assumptions according to probability of actualization and importance.
3. Convert the classification of each assumption into quantitative values (A = 4, E = 3 …); multiply the values, and select the two or three assumptions with highest value.
4. Use the selected assumptions individually or as a group to diversify the basic scenario.

Positive scenarios—Manufacturing Business X:

- The expectation that the existing economic stability will be maintained and the arrangements for reducing bureaucracy and taxes lead to an expectation of sustainable 5% growth

	Very certain	Uncertain
Very important		
Low importance		

Figure 9.2 Certainty–importance grid.

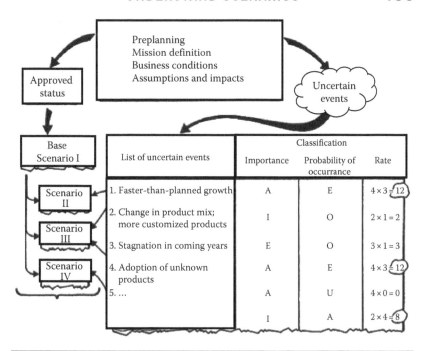

Figure 9.3 Generating scenarios—example.

during the next 5 years. This climate will result in increased foreign direct investments and will be supported.

- As a result of the flow of global liquidity from developed country markets to developing country markets, stable and low-cost interest and exchange rates (particularly in nation), the currently rising young population, and the support of all these factors with the mortgage law prepared by the government, the demand for housing will grow and the construction industry will assume a growth trend above the economic growth.

- As a result of standardization in the industry through laws to be enacted by nations in the EU accession process, traditional methods will be replaced by industrial methods. Thus, the market volume of standardized industrial products will increase and the need for know-how in production will bring about sectorial consolidation.

- It will not be possible to replace advanced technology products, which will emerge as a result of construction technologies following a rapid development trend, with traditional products. Traditional structure will be replaced by rapid and economic solutions to be enabled by new application systems and new strategies enabling direct access to end users.

- The advantages offered by the geographical position of the nation and her active role in regional countries will allow the industry to expand in the region. Domestic contracting companies that have gained a regional company structure will move national construction material manufacturers into a position of regional manufacturers.

Negative scenarios—"Manufacturing Business X":

- Potential negative developments in foreign relations (EU accession process, Cyprus issue, Iraq) will lead to fluctuations and instability in national economy. Such fluctuation in the economy will lead to weakened purchasing power. This contraction in market would negatively affect the construction industry.
- Weakened purchasing power would increase demand for traditional methods and reduce the market of industrial products.
- The ongoing economic program would be interrupted. The country's borrowing costs would increase and expenditures would diminish. Devaluation would be inevitable to overcome this contraction in economy. Devaluation would lead to crisis in sectors using external loans. Furthermore, energy and raw material costs would rise, capacity utilization would decline and prices would surge.

9.3 Opportunities and Threats

The opportunities and threats that may be offered and posed for the business under the positive and negative scenarios to come out from scenario analysis must be identified. Moreover, determining the strengths and weaknesses of the company compared to its competitors will be able to carry the analysis to a satisfactory result. In short, competitive advantages and weaknesses of the business need to be matched with the potential positive (attractive) and negative (risky) scenarios in the industry. Tables 9.1 and 9.2 show matrices of opportunities and threats.

Table 9.1 Matrix of Opportunities

		POSSIBILITY OF SUCCESS	
		HIGH	LOW
APPEAL	HIGH	1	2
	LOW	3	4

Table 9.2 Matrix of Threats

		POSSIBILITY OF REALIZATION	
		HIGH	LOW
RISK	HIGH	1	2
	LOW	3	4

The competitive advantages and the weaknesses when matched with the result of scenarios provide the critical foundation for opportunities and threats formulation.

No. 1: The opportunities in this field are the most appealing ones for the business.

Nos. 2 and 3: The opportunities in this field should be followed for the changes that could develop the possibilities of appeal or success.

No. 4: The opportunities in this field are at insignificant level for the business.

No. 1: As the threats in this field are the ones that could provide the most extensive harm to the business, before their realization, plans should be made for the things to be done.

Nos. 2 and 3: Even if there is no necessity to make assumption plans for the threats in these fields, it should be followed very carefully.

No. 4: Threats in this field are negligible.

While developing strategies for the future, opportunities will have a significant influence while threats will be monitored closely by the business and measures will be taken against them.

Opportunities, by definition, arise in cases where the unresolved problems and unsatisfied expectations and needs are identified for the use of products and/or services in the market, and if solutions can be produced for these.

An opportunity, then, is the possibility to do things both *differently* and *better* than how they are being done at the moment. In economic terms, *differently* might take the form of offering a new product or of organizing the business in a different way. *Better* means the product offers utility in terms of an ability to satisfy human needs, that existing products do not.

9.3.1 Matching Positive Scenarios with Competitive Positions

By testing out total market attractiveness of each positive scenario, you would be able to screen out investment opportunities even before considering what kind of competitive advantages you might be able to attain. The *attractiveness* is the net benefits less the costs (not just the benefits).

Drivers of growth are used for assessing the market attractiveness of a particular positive scenario in Figure 9.4. This is accomplished through vector analysis (where arrows represent strength of growth drivers).

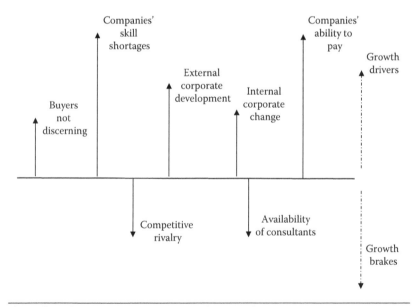

Figure 9.4   Market attractiveness of a scenario—example.

Vector analysis is a way of mapping the impact of forces for growth in an industry. The length of the vector arrow represents the perceived strength of the force driving growth.

As (Ansoff 1970) stated, growth brakes are the forces which throw growth into reverse. To identify the potential growth brakes you need to amplify the *weak signals* concept from the environment. The upwards arrows are growth drivers, the downwards arrows are brakes on growth. A very long downward arrow represents a stopper on growth.

Besides market attractiveness of a scenario, to position a business effectively on the GE grid you also need to take some view of its competitive position with regard to the particular scenario. The following ten key criteria will usually suffice:

- Brand, image, and reputation
- Simplicity of product/market focus, or alternatively a relevant and broad offering
- Relative market (or niche) share
- Product and service performance
- Distribution channels
- Cost base
- Responsiveness (but this does not mean reactiveness)
- Technical and nontechnical competencies
- Financial strength
- Management skills

The aforementioned factors can be scored as *strong*, *average*, or *weak*. Also, the relative importance of the factors can be assessed by weighting some factors as being more important than others.

9.3.2 *Business Opportunities*

Figure 9.5 shows the GE grid that enables you to

- Position a business, having determined market attractiveness of a scenario and competitive position of a business with regard to the particular scenario
- Evaluate business opportunities
- Reposition a business (from right to left on the GE grid, or even [by shifting the business' market focus] diagonally north–west)

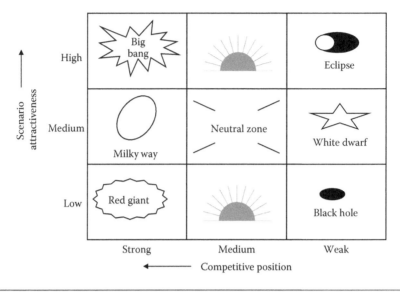

Figure 9.5 Business opportunities. (Rasiel, E.M., *The McKinsey Way*, McGraw-Hill Trade, Columbus, OH, 1999.)

- Challenge the adequacy of investment to achieve such a repositioning (both long-term investment and revenue costs with longer-term benefits)
- Compare your positioning with other key competitors operating in the same or different market segments

Starting at the north-west point, business units with high total market attractiveness and strong competitive position are called *Big Bang* to suggest that they are likely to throw off a lot of cash. Businesses with medium total market attractiveness and a strong position are still likely to generate considerable cash (and earnings). While moving south, a strong position in a low market attractiveness area is more likely to struggle to produce a good profit and cash stream.

Moving to the middle of the GE grid, an average position in a highly attractive market may again be very well rewarded. But this *Sunrise* position may easily slip in terms of the competition position, becoming an *Eclipse* or move into the middle, *Neutral Zone*.

The *Eclipse* is an interesting business position: here a business unit might move out of the dark into a *Sunrise* position. Or, it might be about to fall off the edge of the grid to the right.

At the bottom of the grid, a *Sunset* business (average competitive position in a market with low attractiveness) will probably struggle to make adequate profit and be pushed hard to generate much cash. We call this the *Red Giant* because it is often a substantial business but one that has not got much potential as an opportunity (except through incremental development or by break-out into more attractive niches elsewhere.)

Equally, a weak position in a medium attractive market is also unlikely to generate reasonable financial returns (the *White Dwarf*—this is so named because it is a burnt-out star). A weaker position in a low attractiveness market will invariably lead to financial losses and the need for continual financing. This is called the *Black Hole* of the GE grid.

A special danger is where a business thinks that it will be able to enter the market in the *Big Bang* or *Sunrise* cell of the GE matrix, but actually enters in the *Black Hole* position. Because of lags in recognizing this problem it may be some time before it is reflected in financial results and its root causes are diagnosed, therefore leading to increased, rather than reduced, commitment to this opportunity move.

9.3.3 Screening and Selecting Opportunities

Not all opportunities are equally valuable. A business with limited resources cannot pursue every opportunity with which it is faced. It must select those opportunities that are going to be the most rewarding. The key decisions in screening and selecting opportunities relate to the size of the opportunity, the investment necessary to exploit it, the rewards that will be gained, and the risks likely to be encountered. Specifically, the decision on selecting opportunities, illustrated in Figure 9.6, should be based on the answers to the following questions:

- *Market attractiveness*: Is the market (or segment) inherently attractive (consider key growth drivers and brakes)?
- *Competitive advantage*: Are we likely to have (and be able to sustain) a competitive position?
- *Financial attractiveness*: Are we likely to make enough money out of it?
- *Implementation capability*: Do we have the capability, resources, and commitment to implement it effectively?

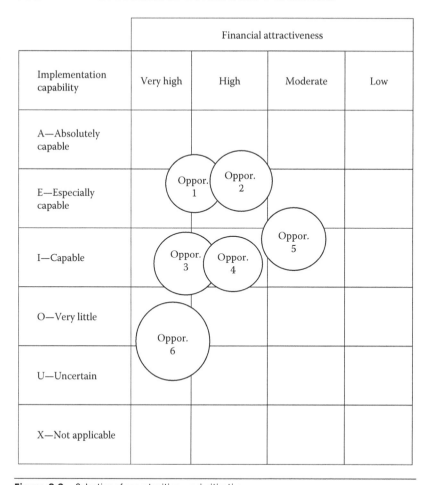

Figure 9.6 Selection of opportunities—prioritization.

For answering the aforementioned questions, you may use quantitative and qualitative approaches.

- Qualitative approach:
  - Who are the customers?
  - How are they differentiated from noncustomers?
  - What needs do these customers have in relation to the product category?
  - How well do consumers find that current offerings satisfy those needs?
  - In what ways are current offerings unsatisfactory?

- What are the customers' attitudes toward the product category in general (positive, negative)?
- Why do noncustomers not use the product category?
- How might they be attracted to it?
- If the product is not valuable, how might other types of product be used as a substitute?
- How does this define a gap for an innovative offering?
- How are they normally informed about the product category?

  The diameter of the circle represents the relative position of an opportunity with respect to the market attractiveness and its competitive position (that is gathered from GE Grid shown in Figure 9.5.)
- Who influences the consumer when they use the product?
- How do they greet innovations in the product category? (Positively or with suspicion?)

- Quantitative approach:
  - How large is the market (its volume)?
  - How much is it worth (its value)?
  - How fast is it growing?
  - How large are the key segments in the market?
  - How many customers are there?
  - How much do they buy?
  - How often do they buy?
  - What are the market shares of the competitors supplying the market?
  - What level of investment do competitors make in developing the market and defending their position with it?

Opportunities—"Manufacturing Business X":

- Increase in foreign investments would boost competitiveness and expand market volume. Furthermore, scenarios reveal that positive conclusions of EU accession process would reduce black cement-based plaster penetration. In the gypsum-based plaster sector, the market volume is expected to reach 8400 Kton by 2014. The anticipated sales quantity in the market is 2500 Kton, which accounts for 24% of the market volume.

Business x will capture a market share of 12% thanks to its advanced R&D, prestigious trademark, experienced staff, and rapid investment capability.

- Increase in foreign investments would boost competitiveness and expand market volume. Furthermore, scenarios reveal that positive conclusions of EU accession process would reduce black cement-based plaster penetration. In the cement-based plaster sector, market volume is expected to reach 36,200 kton by 2014. The anticipated sales of industrial plasters is 525 kton. Business x will capture a market share of 47% in 2011 thanks to its prestigious trademark and experienced staff.

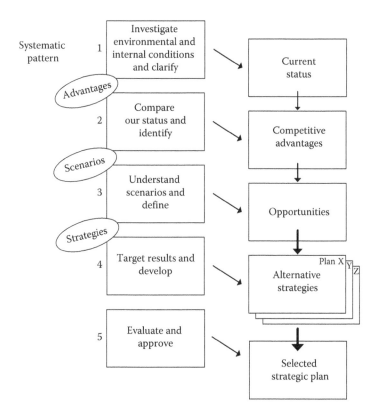

10

STRATEGIC OBJECTIVES, MAIN GOALS, AND MAIN STRATEGIES

It is necessary to always think about the future. Remember that all that's being done is indeed intended to predict the future and focus on the future rather than the present in this section.

The parameters constituting the assumed opportunities need to be laid down as strategic objectives and main goals. Another important point in this section is to avoid selecting too many goals hard to follow and understand.

Furthermore, strategic objectives and main goals should be used for following up the strategies to be developed and the functional plans to be prepared under these strategies.

The things done well and poorly should also be utilized when identifying strategic objectives and main goals.

The following strategic questions need to be answered for *things done well*:

- Can these aspects be improved?
- What needs to be done to improve them?
- What is needed for improvement?
- Do they really create value additions within operations?
- What do they contribute to the business?
- It is performed better than necessary?
- How can it be done at lower cost?
- What would happen in its absence?
- Can it be used for other alternative activities?

The following strategic questions need to be answered for *things done poorly*:

- How can they be done better?
- Can they be eliminated?
- Is it worth eliminating them?
- What is the cost of elimination?

10.1 Strategic Objectives

Strategic objectives are the conceptual results that the business aims at achieving within a certain timeframe. Strategic objectives and main goals answer the question "*what do we want to achieve?*" within the strategic planning system.

A strategic objective demonstrates the point that the business considers attaining within a general framework. Strategic objectives must be designed to further the function of the business and at the same time should be realistic and achievable. Characteristics of strategic objectives:

- Must be consistent with mission, vision, and principles
- Must contribute to the ability of business to fulfill its mission

- Must be ambitious, but realistic and achievable
- Must enable the business to transform from its current status to desired status in the future
- Must clearly express the point desired to be attained, but must not explain in detail how it will be attained
- Must be adaptable for employees so that they comply with the mission of the organization
- Must be shaped according to the priorities of the business
- Must cover a medium-term timeframe
- Must not be modified unless significant external changes occur

Examples of strategic objectives:

- *Southwest*: "Do the right thing"
- *Motorola*: "Total customer satisfaction"

10.2 Main Goals

Main goals are specific and measurable subobjectives specified for achievement of strategic objectives. Unlike strategic objectives, goals are expressed in quantifiable terms and cover a shorter term. Multiple goals may be established to achieve a strategic objective.

Main goals are the qualitative and quantitative expression of strategic objectives within a defined timeframe. For this reason, they are measurable subobjectives intended for outputs to be achieved. Goals should be expressed in terms of quantity, cost, quality, and time.

Furthermore, while establishing main goals, it would be useful to use strengths more efficiently and take measures for compensating the weaknesses.

Financial and market goals:

- Target markets
- Product range
- Sales volume and profitability for the planned period
- Comparative growth expectations
- Countries to operate in
- Regional concentration
- Strategic partnerships considered

Operational goals:

- Organization
- Training and experience
- Wage and compensation
- Investment goals
- Labor turnover rate
- Safety regulations
- Environmental standards
- Technology and equipment choice
- Scrap rates
- Maintenance and repair policies
- Product standards (quality and performance standards)
- Long-term capacity plans
- Labor level
- Production quantities
- Inventory level
- Overtime work
- Subcontractor

Goals must

- Be clear enough and in understandable detail
- Be measurable
- Be ambitious, but not impossible to achieve
- Focus on results
- Have a defined timeframe
- Be consistent and coherent

Benefits of clear goals:

- Provide guidance for planning and implementation
- Help establish synergy or emerge
- Facilitate the establishment of priorities
- Reduce uncertainties
- Eliminate conflicts
- Encourage effort and creativity
- Ensure measurement of success

Decisions regarding identification, control, and rewarding of goals are (Wickham 2004):

- How will goals be established?
- Who will be responsible for establishing goals?
- For whom will goals be established? (Organization, function, teams, or persons?)
- What will be the characteristics of goals? (Financial or strategic?)
- What information will be needed to monitor goals?
- How will achievement of goals be rewarded? What will be done in case of failure?

Questions required to be answered to establish goals:

- Are goals consistent with the mission, vision, policies, and strategic objectives of the business?
- What specific results are intended to be achieved? What are the factors affecting results?
- When the goals for a strategic objective are achieved, can that strategic objective be attained?
- Is there a requirement to achieve the goals within a certain period of time?
- How long will it take to attain the desired results?
- How is the progress toward achieving these goals measured?
- What are the benchmarks? How much progress can be ensured?

Examples of main goals:

- *"Southwest"*:
  Treat employees like number one.
  Offer the lowest ticket fee.
  Offer the highest flight frequency.
  Offer best customer services.
  Recruit best people.
  Enjoy.

- *"Motorola"*:
  Best class of people, marketing, technology, software, and systems.
  Growing global market
  Better financial results
- *"Manufacturing Business X"*:
  Turnover will be 200 million USD, and profitability will be 38 million USD in 2014.
  Entering new markets: Balkans, Russia, Cyprus, Ukraine, and North Africa
  Increasing brand recognition
  Customer relations management and customer-oriented sales
  Developing new products (plaster board, technical mortars, and liquids)
  Making new investments: defined domestic and overseas locations
  Raising productivity to 85% and shortening/speeding up production process through technology investments
  Optimizing and improving costs
  Maintaining/improving product quality and attaining 5 Sigma
  Raising capacity utilization rate to 70%
  Settling the centralized management understanding
  Developing quality management systems
  Settling the performance culture
  Offering opportunities for employees to improve their skills

10.3 Main Strategies

Strategies are instruments for achievement of long-term goals. It is a course of action selected from a series of options in order to achieve a goal established against uncertainties.

It is critical to distinguish between goals and strategies. Goals imply the desired result. Strategy, however, shows how the goal can be achieved. Strategies must be consistent with goals and must enable achievement of goals.

Alternative strategies are developed by searching for an answer to the question *"what should businesses do to be competitive and lasting in their own industries and markets?"*

Determination of a suitable strategy for a business begins in identifying the opportunities and risks in its environment. This (discussion) is concerned with the identification of a range of alternative strategies, the narrowing of this range by recognizing the constraints imposed by business capability, and the determination of one or more strategies at acceptable levels of risk. While evaluating the opportunities defined on the basis of analyses conducted, various strategies we can implement come forth:

- You should have a single strategy for a single opportunity.
- If there are multiple opportunities, you can have multiple strategies.

Based on using both the techniques of *Generic Competitive Strategies* and *Components of Strategy*, described in the following subsections, the main strategy(ies) can be identified. Accordingly, this will lead you to the selection of the corresponding *Grand Strategy(ies)* (described in the following section).

10.3.1 Generic Competitive Strategies*

The fundamental basis of above-average performance in the long run is *sustainable competitive advantage*. There are two basic types of competitive advantage a business can possess: low cost and differentiation. Any strengths or weaknesses are ultimately a function of relative cost or differentiation.

The two basic types of competitive advantage combined with the scope of activities for which a business seeks to achieve them lead to *three generic strategies* for achieving above-average performance in an industry (Table 10.1). Each involves a different route to competitive

Table 10.1 Three Generic Strategies

		COMPETITIVE ADVANTAGE	
		LOW COST	DIFFERENTIATION
SCOPE	BROAD	1. Cost leadership	2. Differentiation
	NARROW	3a. Cost focus	3b. Differentiation focus

Source: Porter, M.E., *Competitive Strategy: Techniques for Analyzing Industries and Competitors*, The Free Press, Florence, 1998.

---

* Descriptions of generic strategies are adapted from Porter (1998).

advantage, combining competitive advantage sought with the scope of the target. The specific actions required to each generic strategy vary widely from industry to industry.

Broad target is defined as one which

1. Covers a great diversity of customer needs and market segments
2. Covers a wide and perhaps complex range of products and services
3. Covers both (1) and (2)

Competitive advantage is at the heart of an industry, and achieving competitive advantage requires a firm to make a choice about the type of competitive advantage it seeks to attain and the scope within which it will attain it. Being all things to all people is below-average performance, which means that a business has no competitive advantage at all.

10.3.1.1 Cost Leadership   A business sets out to become the low-cost producer in its industry. The business serves many industry segments. The sources of cost advantage depend on the structure of the industry and may include the pursuit of economies of scale, proprietary technology, preferential access to raw materials, and other factors.

Low-cost producer status involves more than just going down the learning curve. Low-cost producers typically sell a standard product and place considerable emphasis on cost advantages from all sources.

At equivalent or lower prices than its rivals, a cost leader's low-cost position translates into higher returns. A cost leader cannot ignore the basis of differentiation. If its product is not perceived as comparable or acceptable by buyers, a cost leader will be forced to discount prices well below competitors to gain sales.

The strategic logic of cost leadership usually requires that a business be the cost leader. Unless, a business can gain a cost lead and persuade others to abandon their strategies, the consequences can be disastrous.

Thus, cost leadership is a strategy particularly dependent on preemption, unless major technological change allows a business to radically change its cost position.

10.3.1.2 Differentiation   A business seeks to be unique in its industry along some dimensions. It selects one or more attributes that many buyers in an industry perceive as important, rewarded for its unique-ness with a premium price.

Differentiation can be based on the product itself, the delivery sys-tem by which it is sold, the market approach, and a broad range of other factors.

A business that can achieve and sustain differentiation will be an above-average performer in its industry, irrespective of its cost posi-tion. A differentiator thus aims at cost parity or proximity relative to its competitors, by reducing cost in all areas that do not affect differentiation.

A business must truly be unique at something or be perceived as unique at something or be perceived as unique if it is to expect a pre-mium price. In contrast to cost leadership, there can be more than one successful differentiation strategy in an industry if there are number of attributes that are widely valued by buyers.

10.3.1.3 Focus It rests on the choice of a narrow competitive scope. The focuser selects a segment or group of segments in the industry by optimizing its strategy for the target segments; the focuser seeks to achieve a competitive advantage in its target segments having two variants.

In *cost focus*, a business seeks a cost advantage in its target segment, while in *differentiation focus* a business seeks differentiation in its target segment. The target segments must either have buyers with unusual needs or the production and delivery system that best serves the target segment must differ from that of other industry segments. Cost focus exploits differences in cost behavior in some segments, while differen-tiation focus exploits the special needs of buyers in certain segments.

Competitors may be underperforming in meeting the needs of a particular segment, which opens the possibility for differentiation focus. Broadly targeted competitors may also be over-performing in meeting the needs of a segment, which means that they are bearing higher than necessary cost in serving it. An opportunity for cost focus may be present in just meeting the needs of such a segment and noth-ing more.

If a business can achieve sustainable cost leadership (cost focus) or differentiation (differentiation focus) in its segment and the segment is structurally attractive, then the focuser will be an above-average performer in its industry. Most industries have a variety of segments, and each one that involves a different buyer need or a different production or delivery system is a candidate for a focus strategy.

10.3.1.4 Stuck in the Middle   A business that fails to achieve any of them is *stuck in the middle*. It possesses no competitive advantage, usually a recipe for below-average performance.

If a business that is stuck in the middle is lucky enough to discover a profitable product or buyer, competitors with a sustainable competitive advantage will quickly eliminate the spoils.

A business that is stuck in the middle will earn attractive profits only if the structure of its industry is highly favorable, or if the business is fortunate enough to have competitors that are also stuck in the middle. Usually, however, such a business will be much less profitable than rivals achieving one of the generic strategies. Industry maturity tends to widen the performance differences between businesses with a generic strategy and those that are stuck in the middle.

10.3.2 Components of Strategy

In conjunction with its objectives, the firm may choose one, two, or all of the strategy components with respect to its product-market position. Components of strategy (Ansoff 1970) can be illustrated by means of a matrix shown in Table 10.2.

10.3.3 Grand Strategies*

Grand strategies, often called business strategies, provide basic direction for strategic actions. Grand strategies indicate how long-range

Table 10.2   Components of Strategy

	PRODUCT	
MARKET	PRESENT	NEW
PRESENT	Market Penetration	Product Development
NEW	Market Development	Diversification

Source: Ansoff, I., *Corporate Strategy*, Penguin, London, U.K., 1970.

---

* Descriptions of grand strategies are adapted from Pearce and Robinson (2011).

objectives will be achieved. Thus, a grand strategy can be defined as a comprehensive general approach that guides major actions:

- Are we going to stay in the same ring of value chain? Are we going to continue doing the same work with the same system? (*Constancy*)
- Are we going to enter new business areas with additional functions, products, and/or markets? (*Expansion*)
- Are we going to leave the business completely? Are we going to leave some of the business? (*Reduction*)

Any one of the following 12 principal grand strategies serve as the basis for achieving major long-term objectives of a business, based on outcomes of generic competitive strategies and components of strategies described in the previous subsections.

- Concentration
- Market development
- Product development
- Innovation
- Horizontal integration
- Vertical integration
- Joint venture
- Concentric diversification
- Conglomerate diversification
- Retrenchment/turnaround
- Divestiture
- Liquidation

10.3.3.1 Concentration The most common grand strategy is *concentration* on the current business. The business directs its resources to the profitable growth of a single product, in a single market, and with a single technology. Concentration is typically lowest in risk and in additional resources required. Also based on the known competencies of the business. Negative side, for most companies' concentration tends to result in steady but slow increases in growth and profitability and a narrow range of investment options.

Succeeds for so many businesses, because of the advantages over its more diversified competitors in production skill, market know-how, customer sensitivity, and reputation in the marketplace.

A grand strategy of concentration allows for a considerable range of actions. Broadly speaking, the business can attempt to capture a larger market share by increasing present customers' rate of usage, by attracting competitors' customers, or by interesting nonusers in the product or service. Concentration (increasing use of present products in present markets) involves

- Increasing present customers' rate of usage
  a. Increasing the size of purchase
  b. Increasing the rate of product obsolescence
  c. Advertising other uses
  d. Giving price incentives for increased use
- Attracting competitors' customers
  a. Establishing sharper brand differentiation
  b. Increasing promotional effort
  c. Initiating price cuts
- Attracting nonusers to buy the product
  a. Inducing trial use through sampling, price incentives, and so on
  b. Pricing up or down
  c. Advertising new uses

10.3.3.2 Market Development Market development involves marketing present products, often with only cosmetic modifications, to customers in related market areas by adding different channels of distribution or by changing the content of advertising or the promotional media. Thus, businesses that open branch offices in new cities, states, or countries are practicing market development. Businesses that switch from advertising in trade publications to newspapers or to support their mail-order sales efforts are using a market development approach. Market development (selling present products in new markets) consists of

- Opening additional geographical markets
  a. Regional expansion
  b. National expansion
  c. International expansion
- Attracting other market segments
  a. Developing product versions to appeal to other segments

    b. Entering other channels of distribution

    c. Advertising in other media

10.3.3.3 Product Development Product development involves substantial modification of existing products or creation of new but related items that can be marketed to current customers through established channels. The product development strategy is often adopted either to prolong the life cycle of current products or to take advantage of favorable reputation and brand name. The idea is to attract satisfied customers to new products as a result of their positive experience with the business' initial offering. Product development (developing new products for present markets) includes

- Developing new product features
  a. Adapt (to other ideas, development)
  b. Modify (change color, motion, sound, odor, form, shape)
  c. Magnify (stronger, longer, thicker, extra value)
  d. Minify (smaller, shorter, lighter)
  e. Substitute (other ingredients, process, and power)
  f. Rearrange (other patterns, layout, sequence, components)
  g. Reverse (inside out)
  h. Combine (blend, alloy, assortment, combine units, appeals, and ideas)
- Developing quality variations
- Developing additional models and sizes (product proliferation)

10.3.3.4 Innovation Markets have come to expect periodic changes and improvements in the products offered. As a result, some businesses find it profitable to base their grand strategy on innovation. They seek initially high profits associated with customer acceptance of a new or greatly improved product. Then they shift from innovation to production or market competence, then move on to search for other original or novel ideas, creating a new product life cycle, thereby making any similar existing products obsolete. This approach differs from the product development strategy of extending an existing product's life cycle.

Most growth-oriented businesses appreciate the need to be innovative. Few innovative ideas prove profitable because research, development, and premarketing costs incurred in converting a promising idea into a profitable product are extremely high.

10.3.3.5 Acquisitions   There are four fundamental processes by which acquisitions can help:

1. *By reducing costs*: Does integration reduce overall costs? This may be achieved by eliminating some fixed or overhead costs. It may be gained by achieving some economy of scale in a key functional area. Existing production capacity may be used more efficiently, especially if there is some overcapacity. Sales team may find it relatively easy to add new items to the portfolio they are selling. They may also find it possible to serve additional customers in their area.

2. *By combining and creating knowledge*: Does integration increase the value of the knowledge held by the individual organizations? Does the acquirer understand customers in a way which promises to make the selling of the acquired business's products more effective? Can the two organizations learn key skills from each other, for example, in R&D or in sales?

3. *By capitalizing on relationships*: Does integration take advantage of the relationships enjoyed by one party? Does the acquired business enjoy a particularly valuable relationship with suppliers or distributors? Does the acquired business have access to new geographical areas or to new customer groups? Sure, care must always be taken to ensure that the acquisition process itself does not upset established relationships.

4. *By developing organizational structure*: Does the integration allow the organization as a whole to develop structural advantages? Does it make the business to react more rapidly in producing new products? Does it enable the business to get its products into new areas or to new customer groups?

10.3.3.6 Horizontal Integration   When the long-term strategy of a business is based on growth through the acquisition of one or more similar businesses operating at the same stage of the production market chain, its grand strategy is called *horizontal integration*. Such acquisitions provide access to new markets for the acquiring business and eliminate competitors. For horizontally integrated businesses, the risk stems from the increased commitment to one type of business.

10.3.3.7 Vertical Integration   When the grand strategy of a business involves the acquisition of businesses that either supply the business with inputs (such as raw materials) or serve as a customer for the business' outputs (such as a warehouse for finished products), it is called *vertical integration*. In backward vertical integration, the business acquired operators at an earlier stage of the production/sales process. Forward vertical integration is the acquisition of a business nearer to the ultimate customer.

The acquiring business is able to greatly expand its operations, thereby achieving greater market share, improving economies of scale, and increasing efficiency of capital usage. These benefits are achieved with only moderately increased risk, since the success of the expansion is principally dependent on proven abilities.

Reason for backward integration is the desire to increase the dependability of supply or quality of raw materials or production inputs. It becomes a great concern when the number of suppliers is small and the number of competitors is large. The vertically integrating firm can better control its costs and thereby improve the profit margin of the expanded production/sales system. Forward integration is preferred if the advantages of stable production are particularly high. A business can increase the predictability of demand for its output. For vertically integrated businesses, the risks result from expansion of the business into areas requiring broadening the base of its competencies and responsibilities.

10.3.3.8 Joint Venture   Occasionally, two or more capable businesses lack a necessary component for success in a particular competitive environment. The solution is a set of joint ventures. A particular form of joint venture is joint ownership—domestic businesses to join foreign businesses. This approach presents new opportunities with risks that can be shared. On the other hand, joint ventures often limit partnership, discretion, control, and profit potential while demanding managerial attention, and others that might otherwise be directed toward the mainstream activities of the business.

10.3.3.9 Concentric Diversification   Diversification represents distinctive departures from a business' existing base of operations, typically the acquisition or internal generation of a separate business with synergistic possibilities counterbalancing the two businesses' strengths and weaknesses. However, diversifications are occasionally undertaken as unrelated investments because of their otherwise minimal resource demands and high profit potential.

When diversification involves the addition of a business related to the business in terms of technology, markets, or products, it is concentric diversification. The new businesses selected possess a high degree of compatibility with the current businesses. The ideal occurs when the combined company profits increase strengths and opportunities as well as decrease weaknesses and exposure to risk. Thus, acquiring company searches for new businesses with products, markets, distribution channels, technologies, and resource requirements that are familiar but not identical, synergetic but not wholly interdependent.

10.3.3.10 Conglomerate Diversification   Concern of the acquiring business is the profit pattern of the venture unlike the approach taken in concentric diversification. They may seek a balance in their portfolios between current business with cyclical sales, between high cash/low-opportunity businesses, or between debt-free and highly leveraged businesses.

Concentric acquisitions emphasize some commonality in markets, products, or technology, whereas conglomerate acquisitions are based principally on profit considerations.

10.3.3.11 Retrenchment/Turnaround   A business can find itself with declining profits. Economic recessions, production inefficiencies, and innovative breakthroughs by competitors are the only three causes. The business can survive and eventually recover if a concerted effort is made over a period of a few years to fortify basic distinctive competencies. This type of grand strategy is known as *retrenchment*.

- *Cost reduction*: Examples include decreasing the work force, leasing rather than purchasing equipment, extending the life of machinery, and eliminating elaborate promotional activities.

- *Asset reduction*: Examples include the sale of land, buildings, and equipment not essential to the basic activity of their business.

If these fail to achieve the required reductions, more drastic action may be necessary. It is sometimes essential to lay off employees, drop items from a production line, and even eliminate low-margin customers. The purpose of retrenchment is to reverse current negative trends, and the strategy is often referred to as a *turnaround* strategy. Bringing in new managers was believed to introduce new perspectives, to raise employee morale, and to facilitate drastic actions, such as deep budgetary cuts in established programs.

10.3.3.12 Divestiture A divestiture strategy involves the sale of a business or a major business component. Because the intent is to find a buyer willing to pay a premium above the value of fixed assets for a going concern, the term "sale for market" is more appropriate. Prospective buyers must be convinced that because of their skills and resources, or the synergy with their existing businesses, they will be able to profit from the acquisition.

Often, they arise because of partial mismatches between the acquired business and the parent corporation. Mismatched parts cannot be integrated into the corporation's mainstream. Second reason is the corporation's financial needs. Sometimes, the cash flow or financial stability of the corporation as a whole can be greatly improved if businesses with high market value can be sacrificed.

10.3.3.13 Liquidation When the grand strategy is that of liquidation, the business is typically sold in parts, only occasionally as a whole, but for its tangible asset value and not as a going concern. A business admits failure and recognizes that this action is likely to result in great hardships to itself and its employees. For these reasons, liquidation is usually seen as the least attractive of all grand strategies. However, as a long-term strategy it minimizes the loss to all stakeholders of the business. Usually faced with bankruptcy, the liquidation business tries to develop a planned and orderly system that will result in the greatest possible return and cash conversion as the business slowly relinquishes its market share. Planned liquidation can be worthwhile.

Grand strategies—Manufacturing Business X:

- Domestic:

	CONCENTRATION	MARKET DEVELOPMENT	PRODUCT DEVELOPMENT	HORIZONTAL INTEGRATION
ABS	A + B + C	A	A + B	A
CBS	A + C	B	B	

- Concentration
  - A. Doing business in existing markets with existing products
  - B. Ensuring that existing customers are utilized at a greater scale
  - C. Making the customers without any consumption habit yet ready for consumption
- Market development
  - A. Offering existing products to new markets
  - B. Entering new segments as market
- Product development
  - A. Adding new features to existing products
  - B. Improving the quality structure of existing products
- Horizontal integration
  - A. Acquisition of competitors
- Overseas:
  - Investing/purchasing in regions with security and strategic importance
  - Establishing joint ventures with strong companies in their region or opening branches/leasing

11

EVALUATE ALTERNATIVE STRATEGIC PLANS

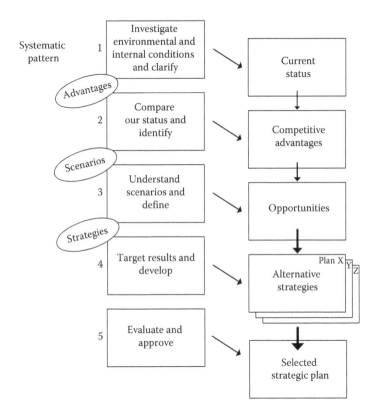

Here, the most suitable strategic plan can be selected for the business. To do this, the alternative strategies are evaluated, which are developed in the previous section for the correspondent opportunities. In order to get best decision, evaluation should be made objectively and impartially as possible. The following techniques that may be applied simultaneously or interchangeably to select the best of alternative strategies:

- Factors analysis
- Strategic option grid
- Risk drivers

Even if the best strategy is selected by any of these techniques described later, contingency plans are still necessary for the selected strategy in a risky environment. A sensitivity analysis needs to be conducted, taking into consideration the possibility that basic assumptions and parameters do not come out as expected and the measures considered to be taken in this respect need to be identified.

11.1 Factors Analysis

Factors analysis, which is generated by Muther (2011), can prevent your overlooking an important factor. Besides, it allows you to let the key users and approvers get into the decision making. Figure 11.1 is a typical factors analysis form.

Ratings should be done by several persons, and each makes his own ratings independent of the others. Then, they can get together to compare the results and resolve any differences.

- Identify each alternative and label the alternatives with letters.
- Establish all pertinent factors, considerations, or objectives affecting the choice of the best alternative.
- Assign to each factor a weight value indicating its relative importance to the strategy's effectiveness. Select the most important factor and assign to it a weight of 10. Select the least and assign it a low number like 1, 2, or 3. Weigh the importance to the factor relative to the most important (10) and the least important.
- Rate for each factor the effectiveness of each alternative strategy in achieving that factor's objective—using A, E, I, and O to represent a descending order of effectiveness. Work across the form from side to side rather than from top to bottom in each column. By doing this, you can be sure to keep the same meaning for a given factor as you move from strategy to strategy.

				Description of Alternatives:					
				X.						
EVALUATING DESCRIPTION				Y.						
A = Almost Perfect, O = Ordinary Result				Z.						
E = Especially Good, U = Unimportant/Result				V.						
I = Important Result, X = Not Acceptable				W.						

	FACTOR/CONSIDERATION	WT	ALTERNATIVE				
			X	Y	Z	V	W
1.							
2.							
3.							
4.							
5.							
6.							
7.							
8.							
9.							
10.							
TOT.	**Weighted Rated Down Total**						

a. _____   d. _____

b. _____   e. _____

c. _____   f. _____

Figure 11.1   Factors analysis form. (Muther, R., *Planning by Design*, Institute for High Performance Planners, Kansas City, MO, 2011.)

- Convert all letter ratings to numbers (A = 4, E = 3, I = 2, O = 1), and multiply by the previously established weights.
- Total the weighted rate values for each alternative. The highest total should indicate the best available alternative.

If the winning alternative is not clearly evident (more than the dispersion 12%–15%), there are several things you can do. First, you can re-evaluate with more, or more precise, factors. Second, you can re-evaluate by inviting other people to participate in the ratings.

11.2 Strategic Option Grid

For prioritizing mutually exclusive strategies and for evaluating different strategies based on defined criteria, strategic option grid is used. Figure 11.2 shows a strategic options grid that can be used. Each criteria need to be rated in terms of its attractiveness to the alternative as

- High
- Medium
- Low

You need to reverse the ratings of uncertainty and difficulty.

11.3 Risk Drivers

It is necessary to review the main risks envisaged during the period of strategic plan. Alternative strategies are ranked from least to most risky (considering the probability of actualization). Figure 11.3 shows a certainty–importance grid.

OPTIONS CRITERIA	OPTION 1	OPTION 2	OPTION 3	OPTION 4
Strategic attractiveness				
Financial attractiveness				
Implementation difficulty				
Uncertainty and risk				
Acceptability (to stake holders)				

Figure 11.2   Strategic option grid.

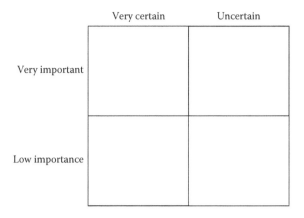

Figure 11.3   Certainty–importance grid.

The probability of actualization should be determined by evaluating the profitability of alternative strategies and the risk factors from which they are affected. The probability of actualization an alternative, within the framework of plans, is determined by reviewing its overall impacts on labor force, management, clients, and level of profitability. The answer to the question "which risk factors affect the profitability of alternative?" may be as follows:

11.3.1 Systematic Risks

These are the risks posed by changes in economic, political, and other environmental conditions. They are risks originating from changes in interest rate, while production and prices are at their normal levels, affecting investment instruments in the same direction but at various degrees.

Sources of systematic risks that are not possible to be kept under control and eliminated

- Changes on the purchasing power
- Changes on the interest rates
- Changes on supply and demand

11.3.2 Nonsystematic Risks

These are risks of changes that affect capital market independently and are not systematic. Nonsystematic risks, which relate to only an industry and business, vary from one industry to other and from one business to other. The nonsystematic risk of each instrument is different since it originates from the characteristics of the business that the investment instrument represents as well as from its specific circumstances. These are as follows:

- Industry risks
- Financial risks
- Managerial risks

While it is impossible to control systematic risk, it is possible to control and eliminate nonsystematic risks whose sources are mentioned previously.

PART IV

IMPLEMENTATION AND CONTROL PHASE

The final phase—planning the detailed arrangement of the strategic plan—is discussed here.

12

IMPLEMENTATION PLAN

The implementation plan required to be created to answer the question "how can we reach our target destination?" in the systematic of strategic planning must be coherent with the whole of strategic plan and be open to mutual interaction.

The business will explain the main strategy for each strategic objective and goals in detail under this heading and will describe the activities and projects required for the realization of this strategy in detail.

This is the phase when action plans are prepared to identify by whom, how, and when the strategy created to achieve strategic objective and goals will be implemented within the business, the action plans created are communicated and implemented within the business.

The roles, responsibilities, and powers of units in charge of implementing the strategy, that is, providing the service, will be defined clearly within the organization during this phase.

The business has to make a prioritization during this implementation phase. After describing the goals prioritized, assigned to responsible units, the activities and projects required to achieve these goals will be explained here in the order of priority.

This phase also involves the preparation of budgets for the utilization of resources required for the realization of action plans (it must be remembered that the strategy has to be discussed and improved continuously, and necessary arrangements must be made in the action plans and budgets accordingly).

The current status and potential of resource/expenditure structure will be taken into consideration. During prioritization, the principles of sustainability, efficiency, productivity, level of impact and relevance will also be taken into consideration. Figure 12.1 illustrates this situation.

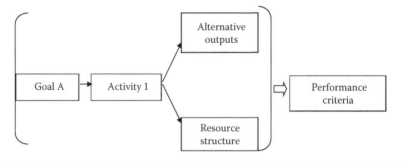

Figure 12.1   Goal, activity, output, and performance relationship.

Note, however, that businesses should shape their budget structures by taking as a basis their strategic plans.

After expressing each goal in activities, activities must be linked to the budget. Figure 12.2 illustrates such a worksheet. The main purpose here is to be able to measure the cost of each activity, by laying down the resource and cost structure during the budget preparation process, as well as to assist the process of prioritizing expenditures.

Annual implementation portions of strategic plan will be identified and reported. The linkage between strategic plan and budgets will assume clarity through these documents. Thus, budgets will be able to support performance implementation.

Key questions required to be answered during the identification of activities:

- What is the role and importance of the activity in the process of achieving the goal?
- Have the way and techniques to be followed for the achievement of goals been defined?

STRATEGIC OBJECTIVE1 GOAL 1.1 ACTIVITIES	CURRENT YEAR (t)	BUDGET YEAR (t + 1)	FOLLOWING FIRST YEAR (t + 2)	FOLLOWING SECOND YEAR (t + 3)
Activity 1.1.1				
Activity 1.1.2				
Activity 1.1.3				
Activity 1.1.4				
...				

Figure 12.2   Activity-cost worksheet.

- On which measurable criteria (forming the basis of performance criteria) are they based?
  - Timing
  - Quantity
  - Cost
  - Quality
- Which units are in charge of achieving the goals and performing the activities under the goals, and what are their responsibilities?
- Have alternative activities to achieve the same goal been identified and discussed?

Factors to be considered in identifying and implementing activities:

- Activities and projects interacting with each other must be properly placed and timing must be established accordingly.
- Each activity must be oriented toward a specific goal.
- They must not overlap with other projects and goals.
- The business most adopt an approach that considers not only the present time and current state, but also medium and long-term expectations and changes, when identifying and implementing the activities and projects. Note, however, that interruption or failure of short-term or annual implementation would negatively affect the implementation of strategy.
- While designing the implementation phase, the units to implement the projects and activities must be identified and the assigned authorities and responsibilities must be clear.
- While implementing activities and projects, it is important to ensure cooperation and coordination between other businesses and related parties.

Dissemination

A success beyond expectations can be achieved when business goals are reduced from the highest level of the organization to the lowest levels successfully and are disseminated to all related activities horizontally.

In this phase, the strategic plan must be disseminated to all levels of the business and shared. A significant portion of strategic plan should be expanded by following a top-down approach hierarchically.

The expansion of goals must cover all hierarchical levels of the business vertically and must be disseminated to all related areas and activities horizontally. During the top-down expansion of strategic plan, the results intended to be achieved in any level must constitute a goal for the immediate lower level.

The expansion of goals in any level must be intended to achieve the immediate higher goal. Department goals must be identified accordingly and individual goals must be explained.

13

MONITORING AND EVALUATION

Systematic strategic planning has a dynamic and continuous character. Any major change in any of the sections making up the systematic may require a series of changes in other sections of the systematic. For instance, a major change in the economic circumstances of the country may pose a threat or offer an opportunity for the long-term goals of the business, eventually requiring the business to change its long-term goals and strategy.

Monitoring is the regular follow-up and reporting of the progress toward goals specified in the strategic plan. Evaluation is the measurement of implementation results against strategic objective and goals and analysis of the consistency and relevance of these objective and goals.

In addition, plan realizations are reported annually during the implementation phase of the strategic plan. During the strategic planning process, feedback is provided using the information obtained as a result of monitoring and evaluation activities. Review of strategic plan involves the comparison of the results targeted and attained. Plan realizations are reviewed in terms of timing and relevance for goals. As a result of this review and evaluation, the plan is confirmed and implementation continues if

- There is no fundamental change in the capacity of the business or in the external environment in which the business performs its operations
- Strategies, action plans, and activities are implemented as planned
- Progress toward achievement of strategic objectives and goals is in line with expectations

On the other hand, if changes are observed in terms of the aforementioned considerations, unexpected, or undesired results are coming about or existing strategic objectives and goals are not realistic, then the plan is revised, re-evaluated and is continues to be implemented with its updated version.

Effective implementation of monitoring and evaluation activities requires linking the goals established in the strategic plan to objective and measurable indicators before proceeding into implementation phase.

Monitoring and evaluation process ensures that activities are constantly improved. It is imperative that the activities covered by the strategic plan are subject to monitoring and evaluation. Otherwise, problems would be faced in enabling the accountability of related parties, in which case strategic plan would not go any further from just being a document. Basic questions in monitoring and evaluation are as follows:

- What did we do?
- How do we understand that we have achieved?
- How effective is implementation?
- What should be changed?

13.1 Monitoring

Monitoring activity consists of the regular reporting of progress toward achievement of objective and goals and its submission to related parties and officials within the business for assessment.

Monitoring is a systematic activity assisting the management. Reports are used in monitoring; furthermore, it focuses mainly on resources, activities and outputs.

Reporting is the primary instrument of monitoring activity. The contents of reports, the frequency by which they will be prepared, the units by which they will be prepared and the authorities to whom they will be presented have to be identified. A monitoring report must contain the following elements:

- Strategic objectives
- Goals
- Activities and projects
- Explanations and comments about realizations
- Information about the current status

Besides enabling the management to evaluate strategic objective and goals, monitoring report would help taking measures rapidly and effectively against unexpected cases.

In addition to areas where progress has been achieved, the issues on which progress could not be achieved must also be reported.

13.2 Evaluation

Evaluation is a comparative analysis of implementation results and predefined strategic objectives and goals. This process essentially involves performance measurement and evaluation.

Performance measurement and evaluation involve determining the extent by which the actualized results overlap with the predefined strategic objectives and goals. Performance measurement and evaluation include the following:

- Ensure effectiveness of management
- Help measureable goals be achieved more easily
- Improve the quality of services
- Is helpful in development and review of budget
- Help answer the question why resources are spent for these activities
- Form the basis of accountability and performance audit

Performance measurement is the measurement of implementation results using performance indicators. The activities required for the realization of strategies must be implemented through mobilization of resources and following a disciplined and organized approach and a close coordination must be ensured among all responsible persons for the success of strategic plan.

Deviations from goals must be identified by following up the performance indicators and the reasons of these deviations must be analyzed. Corrective actions must be discussed and decided. Based on the results obtained, necessary revisions must be made to performance assessments, budget, activities, and strategic plan.

Processes and subprocesses are meaningful if they are measurable and monitor able. For example, when the phrase high product quality is used alone, it is not possible to determine the actual level of product quality, the level of quality intended to be attained and whether progress or improvement has been achieved.

Therefore, critical performance indicators must be defined for each process and subprocess. These indicators must not be hard and expensive to monitor in practice. Too many or hard-to-understand indicators must not be selected.

Performance indicators are instruments that ensure the measurement of the success of strategic plan and implementation results in particular. Performance indicators are used to measure and evaluate the results attained in the process of achieving the strategic objectives and goals of the business and form the basis of performance audit.

A performance indicator is expressed in terms of time, quantity, quality, and cost in order to ensure its measurability. Performance indicators are categorized as input, output, productivity, result, and quality indicators.

Input:

It is the financial and physical resources needed for the production of a good or service. Input indicators reflect the baseline status taken as a basis for measurement. For example,

- "Quantity of spare parts to be used for maintenance and repair."
- "Number of teachers needed."

Output:

It is the quantity of goods or services produced. Although output indicators provide information about the quantity of goods and services produced, they are not descriptive alone as regards whether objectives and goals have been achieved or the quality of goods or services produced and efficiency of production process. For example,

- "Number of machines maintained and repaired."
- "Number of orders processed during a certain period of time."

Productivity:

It represents the input or cost per output. It shows the linkage between inputs and outputs. For example,

- "Maintenance and repair cost per unit of machinery (cost/output.)"
- "Time passed for each order processed (time/output.)"

Result:

Result indicators demonstrate how and to what extent the outputs obtained have been successful in achieving the strategic objective and goals. The level of success in achieving the targeted results is expressed by effectiveness. Result indicators are the most important performance indicators since they reveal whether the strategic objective and goals have been achieved. For example,

- "Improvement in production of machinery maintained (time saved, etc.)"
- "Increase in foreign capital entering and actually invested in the country"

Quality:

The level attained in responding to the expectations of the beneficiaries of goods or services or measures like reliability, honesty, behavioral pattern, sensitivity, and integrity. For example,

- "The ratio of machinery which do not requires maintenance and repair again within a specific period of time to the machinery maintained and repaired"
- "Percentage of the error-free data in the data uploaded to a database"

In principle, at least one input, output, productivity, result, and quality indicator must be defined for each goal. The quality of goals affects the quality of performance indicators as well. Another factor that must be considered in performance evaluation is the linkage of outputs to activities and the relevance of results for strategic objectives.

The creation and evaluation of performance indicators is only possible through obtainment of appropriate data and statistics. The availability of relevant, correct and consistent data is a *sin qua non* precondition for the creation of performance indicators and measurement and evaluation of performance. Questions like the types of data needed, the way how they will be obtained, how, by whom and by how often they will be provided and the constraints to be faced in this process need to be answered.

Performance indicators—*PxD* (*Planning by Design*) *Institute*:

- *Strategic Objective*: "Provide vocational skills to the students who could not enter university by acting in cooperation with the industry"
- *Goal*: "Attain an employment rate of 90% among the graduates of institute in the region by the end of 2014"
- *Input*: "The quantity of teachers, buildings and materials needed for the institute"
- *Output*: "The number of female and male students graduating from the institute"
- *Result*: "Increase in the rate of individuals equipped with vocational skills in the target population"
- *Productivity*: "Cost per trainee"
- *Quality*: "The rate of trainees rating the contents/activities of Institute as minimum 9 on a scale of 10"

Characteristics of indicators:

- Relevance (Is it directly relevant for the strategic objective and goals?)
- Comprehensiveness (Does it cover all aspects of strategic objective and goals?)
- Validity (Does it directly represent the goals that they are intended to measure?)
- Coherence (Can multiple indicators be used together coherently?)
- Objectivity (Is the definition of indicator clear for everyone?)
- Simplicity (Is it easy to calculate and interpret?)
- Reliability (Is the data set correct, consistent and comparable in time?)
- Accessibility (Can data be collected easily, within a short period of time at affordable cost?)
- Practicability (Will the data collected be effective in the decision-making process?)
- Ownership (Do related parties find the use of this indicator relevant?)

Appendix A: Sample Applications

A.1 Company X

Vision:
To become a totally respected regional company for the ones looking for a breathing space and/or trying to carry themselves to a better mood by capturing and influencing the imaginations.

Mission:
To be a continual challenger against the leaders of the entertainment industry and make the consumers' moods better by sensorial joy assets.

A.1.1 Internal Analysis

Table A.1 shows the functional approach worksheet. In the table,

- The strengths are marked as (+)
- The weaknesses are marked as (–)

A.1.2 Environmental Analysis

A.1.2.1 Macroeconomic Analysis Figure A.1 shows macroeconomic analysis table that summarizes the status of the variables with respect

Table A.1   Functional Approach Worksheet

		STRENGTHS/ WEAKNESSES
Marketing	Firm's products /services; breadth of product line	+
	Concentration of sales in a few products or to a few customers	−
	Ability to gather needed information about markets	−
	Market share or submarket shares	−
	Product/service mix and expansion potential	+
	Channels of distribution: number, coverage, and control	−
	Effective sales organization	+
	Product/service image, reputation, and quality	+
	Imaginative, efficient and effective sales promotion, and advertising	−
	Pricing strategy and pricing flexibility	−
	Procedures for digesting market feedback and developing new products, services or markets	+
	After-sale service and follow-up	−
	Goodwill/brand loyalty	−
Finance and Accounting	Ability to raise short-term capital	+
	Ability to raise long-term capital: debt/equity	−
	Corporate-level resources	−
	Cost of capital relative to industry and competitors	−
	Tax considerations	−
	Relations with owners, investors, and stockholders	+
	Leverage positions	+
	Cost of entry and barriers to entry	+
	Price-earnings ratio	+
	Working capital; flexibility of capital structure	−
	Effective cost control, ability to reduce costs	+
	Financial size	−
	Efficient and effective accounting system for cost, budget, and profit planning	+
Production/Operations/ Technical	Raw materials cost and availability	−
	Inventory control systems; inventory turnover	
	Location of facilities; layout and utilization of facilities	−
	Economies of scale	+
	Technical efficiency of facilities and utilization of capacity	−
	Effective use of subcontracting	+

(*Continued*)

Table A.1 (*Continued*) Functional Approach Worksheet

		STRENGTHS/ WEAKNESSES
	Degree of vertical integration, value-added and profit margin	+
	Efficiency and cost/benefit of equipment	+
	Effective operation control procedures	+
	Cost and technological competencies relative to industry and competitors	−
	Research and development/technology/innovation	+
	Patents, trademarks and similar legal protection	+
Personnel	Management personnel	+
	Employees' skill and morale	−
	Labor relations compared to industry and competition	+
	Efficient and effective personnel policies	+
	Effective use of incentives to motivate performance	+
	Ability to level peaks and valleys of employment	+
	Employee turnover and absenteeism	+
	Specialized skills	+
	Experience	−
Organization and General Management	Organizational structure	+
	Firm's image and prestige	
	Firm's record for achieving objectives	+
	Organization of communication system	+
	Overall organizational control system	+
	Organizational climate, culture	+
	Use of systematic procedures and techniques in decision making	+
		−
	Top-management skill, capacities, and interest	+
	Strategic planning system	+
	Intraorganizational synergy	+

to customers, government, finance institutions, suppliers, shareholders, and employees point of views. If macroeconomic factor will

- Turn into a better condition than now, then mark as +
- Remain unchanged, then mark as blank
- Turn into a worse condition than now, and then mark as −

From the customers point of view, the following points are considered:

- Demographical and technological factors will change in a better way.

	Population growth	Age pattern	Immigration trends	Birth and death ratios	Education level	Change in GDP	Income distribution	Interest rates	Supply of cash	Inflation rate	Unemployment rate	Foreign exchange policy	Saving consuming trends	Tax laws	Laws against monopolization	Incentives	Green laws	Business law	Political stability	R&D expenditures	Innovation opportunities	New products	Acceleration - tech. change	Fastness product supply	Increase in automation	Changes in life styles	Expectancy for career	Change in family structure	Changes in personal values
	DEMOGRAPH					ECONOMIC								JUDICIAL - POLITICAL						TECHNOLOGICAL						SOCIO - CULTURAL			
CUSTOMERS	+	+	+	+	+		-	-	-	-	+	-	+	-	+	+	+	+		+	+	+	+	+	+	+	+		
GOVERNMENT	+	-	-	+	+		-	+	-	-	-	+	+	+	+	+	+	+	+	+	+	+	+	+	+	+		-	-
FINANCIAL INSTITUTIONS	+	-	+	+	-	+		-	+	-	-			+	+	+	+	+		+	+	+	+	+	+	+	+	+	+
SUPPLIERS	+	-	+	+	+		-	+	-	-	-	+	+	-	+	+	+	-		+	+	+	+	+			+	+	+
SHARE HOLDERS	-			+	+		+	-	-	-			+	+	-		+	+	+		+	+	+	+	+	+	+	+	+
EMPLOYEES	-	-	-	-	-	+		-	+	-	-	-	-	+	-	+	+	+	+	-		+	+	+		-	-	-	
RESULT																													

	Change for the better
+	Change for the better
	Same as before
-	Change for the worse

Figure A.1 Macroeconomic analysis table.

- Economic factors, except unemployment rate and saving/consuming trends, will be worse.
- The change in GDP will be stable.
- Legal and political factors, except tax laws, will be better and there will be political stability.
- Socio and cultural factors, such as life styles and career expectancy, will be better than now.
- Family structures and personnel values/beliefs will remain unchanged.

From the government point of view, the following points are considered:

- Demographical factors, except age pattern and immigration trends, will be better.
- Economic factors except interest rates, foreign-exchange policy, and saving/consuming trends will be worse.
- The change in GDP will remain unchanged.
- Legal and political factors, except tax laws, and technological factors will be better.
- There would not be change in tax laws.
- Socio and cultural factors, such as family structures and personnel values/beliefs, will be worse than now.
- Change in life styles will remain unchanged.

From the financial institution's point of view, the following points are considered:

- Demographical factors, except age pattern and education level, will be better.
- Economic factors, except interest rates, inflation rate, and unemployment rate, will be better.
- The foreign-exchange policy and income distribution will remain unchanged.
- Legal and political factors, except business law and technological factors will be better.
- There would not be change in business law.
- All socio and cultural factors will be better than now.

From the supplier's point of view, the following points are considered:

- Demographical factors, except age pattern, will be better.
- Economic factors except interest rates, foreign-exchange policy, and saving/consuming trends will be worse.
- The change in GDP will remain unchanged.
- Legal and political factors, except business and tax laws, will be better.
- Socio and cultural factors, except career expectancy, will be better than now.
- Technological factors will be better.

From the shareholder's point of view, the following points are considered:

- Demographical factors, except population growth, will be better.
- Age pattern and immigration trends of the population will remain unchanged.
- Economic factors, except income distribution, foreign-exchange policy, and saving/consuming trends, will be worse.
- The unemployment rate and GDP will remain unchanged.
- Legal and political factors, except tax laws, will be better.
- Law against monopolization and political stability will not change.
- All technological and socio/cultural factors will be better than now.

From the employee's point of view, the following points are considered:

- All demographical factors will be worse.
- Economic factors, except GDP, interest rates and saving/consuming trends, will be worse.
- Legal and political factors, except tax laws and political stability, will be better.
- Technological factors, except research and development expenditures, innovation opportunities and new products, will be worse than now.
- Socio and cultural factors, except changes in life style, will be worse.

A.1.2.2 Competition Analysis The competition analysis table in Figure A.2 shows the status of the existing firms, threats of new companies, competitive power of customers and suppliers.

Rivalry

- Number of firms in the industry is few.
- Industry growth rate is uniform.
- Product differences and specialties are high.
- Fixed costs of the firms are high and cost of leaving industry is reasonable.

	FIRMS IN THE INDUSTRY					THREATS OF NEW COMPANIES						COMPETITIVE POWER OF CUSTOMERS						COMPETITIVE POWER OF SUPPLIERS				
	Quantity of firms in the industry	Growth rate of the industry	Differences and the specialties of the products	Fixed costs	Cost to leave the industry	Costs of the companies in the industry related with the company size	Firms which have the customer-firm loyalty	The equity needed to enter the industry	Ability to reach channel of distribution	Cost advantage related with experience	Barriers to enter the industry	The share of the customer in the whole sale	Potential of production of the products by integration	Alternative suppliers	Cost of the change of the suppliers	Flexibility in the prices	The importance of the product for the customers	Quantity of firms in the industry and the production place	Unique products sale	Substitute goods in the market	Potential of production of the products by integration	The share of the sale of the supplier
High	0	0	1	1	0	0	0	1	1	0	0	0	0	0	1	0	0	0	1	1	0	0
Avg.	0	1	0	0	1	1	0	0	0	1	0	0	1	0	0	1	0	0	0	0	1	1
Low	1	0	0	0	0	0	1	0	0	0	1	1	0	1	0	0	1	1	0	0	0	0

Figure A.2 Macroeconomic analysis table.

New players

- High capital investment is necessary to enter into the industry.
- Hard to reach to the channels of distribution.

Customers and suppliers

- Cost of changing suppliers is high.
- Prices are flexible.
- Number of suppliers is few.

A.1.2.3 Industry Life Cycle Due to its dependency on technological development, new segments of media and entertainment industry are constantly being introduced. Entertainment and media is evolved in a highly dynamic nature. Entertainment and media industry revenues were $1.321.890 billion in 2009, grew further to $1.356.574 billion in 2010, and it is expected to be $1.690.298 billion in 2014 globally.

Internet advertising will be the fastest growing media during the next 5 years. Advertising will increase from $2.005 billion in 2010 to $3.148 billion in 2014 in Turkey. Our industry is in a growth stage (as shown in Figure A.3).

A.1.3 Competitive Advantages, Success Factors, Weaknesses

Table A.2 is a comparison table that ends-up with competitive advantages, success factors and weaknesses of the firm. In short, we can say that

- *Competitive advantages*: Factors providing the business with an edge compared to its main competitor and industry average, that is, the ones that have plus sign only on the Co. X column.

		2009	Increase (%)	2010	Increase (%)	2014* (foresight)
Complete Entertainment and Media Industry (trillion $)	Turkey	5.264	11,36	5.862	65,17	9.682
	Global	1.321.890	2,62	1.356.574	24,60	1.690.298
Internet access (billion $)	Turkey	1.457	19,35	1.739	109,20	3.638
	Global	228.060	8,50	247.453	41,88	351.095
Advertising (billion $)	Turkey	1.741	15,16	2.005	57,01	3.148
	Global	405.582	0,91	409.278	21,59	497.648
Consumer/end-user spending (billion $)	Turkey	2.066	2,52	2.118	36,73	2.896
	Global	688.248	1,68	699.843	20,25	841.555

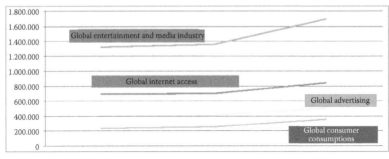

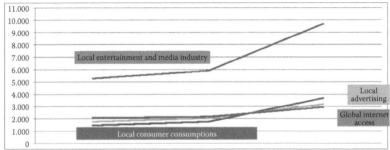

Figure A.3   Industry life cycle.

Table A.2 Comparison Table

		INDUSTRY	MAIN COMPETITOR	CO. X
Marketing	Firm's products/services; breadth of product line	+	+	+
	Concentration of sales in a few products or to a few customers	−	−	−
	Ability to gather needed information about markets	−	−	−
	Market share or submarket shares	+	+	−
	Product/service mix and expansion potential	−	−	+
	Channels of distribution: number, coverage and control	+	+	−
	Effective sales organization	−	+	+
	Product/service image, reputation and quality	+	+	+
	Imaginative, efficient and effective sales promotion and advertising	−	−	−
	Pricing strategy and pricing flexibility	−	−	−
	Procedures for digesting market feedback and developing new products, services or markets	+	+	+
	After-sale service and follow up	−	−	−
	Goodwill/brand loyalty	−	−	−
Finance and Accuonting	Ability to raise short-term capital	−	+	+
	Ability to raise long-term capital: debt/equity	−	+	−
	Corporate-level resources	−	−	−
	Cost of capital relative to industry and competitors	+	+	−
	Tax considerations	−	−	−
	Relations with owners, investors and stockholders	+	+	+
	Leverage positions	+	+	+
	Cost of entry and barriers to entry	+	+	+
	Price-earnings ratio	−	+	+
	Working capital; flexibility of capital structure	−	+	−
	Effective cost control, ability to reduce costs	−	−	+
	Financial size	+	+	−
	Efficient and effective accounting system for cost, budget, and profit planning	−	+	+
Production/Technical	Raw materials cost and availability	−	−	−
	Inventory control systems; inventory turnover	−	−	−
	Location of facilities; layout and utilization of facilities	+	+	+

(*Continued*)

Table A.2 (*Continued*)   Comparison Table

		INDUSTRY	MAIN COMPETITOR	CO. X
	Economies of scale	−	+	−
	Technical efficiency of facilities and utilization of capacity	−	−	−
	Effective use of subcontracting	−	−	+
	Degree of vertical integration, value added and profit margin	+	+	+
	Efficiency and cost/benefit of equipment	+	+	+
	Effective operation control procedures	+	+	+
	Cost and technological competencies relative to industry and competitors	−	+	−
	Research and development/technology/ innovation	−	+	+
	Patents, trademarks and similar legal protection	+	+	+
Paersonnel	Management personnel	−	−	+
	Employees' skill and morale	+	+	−
	Labor relations compared to industry and competition	−	−	+
	Efficient and effective personnel policies	+	+	+
	Effective use of incentives to motivate performance	+	+	+
	Ability to level peaks and valleys of employment	−	−	+
	Employee turnover and absenteeism	+	+	+
	Specialized skills	−	+	+
	Experience	−	−	−
Organization and General Management	Organizational structure	+	+	+
	Firm's image and prestige	−	+	+
	Firm's record for achieving objectives	+	+	+
	Organization of communication system	+	+	+
	Overall organizational control system	−	−	+
	Organizational climate, culture	+	+	+
	Use of systematic procedures and techniques in decision making	−	−	−
	Top-management skill, capacities, and interest	−	−	+
	Strategic planning system	+	−	+
	Intraorganizational synergy	+	−	+

- *Success factors*: Factors that are important capabilities for the business to have but are also typical of every viable competitor; does not represent a potential source of any strategic advantage.
- *Key vulnerabilities*: Factors on which the business currently lacks the necessary skill, knowledge, or resources to compete effectively, and shown as minus sign on the Co. X column.

A.1.4 Scenarios and Opportunities

A.1.4.1 Positive and Negative Scenarios   Positive scenarios include the following:

- Product/service mix and expansion potential: The industry is new and yet products are highly demanded.
- Product/service image, reputation and quality: Despite the intensive use of technology, a lot of work is based on creativity so there will be many opportunities to offer quality products to the market.
- Ability to raise short-term capital: Investors are willing to invest this technology-intensive, promising, and rapidly growing industry.
- Cost of entry and barriers to entry is high for new players.

Negative scenarios include the following:

- In media and especially in animation sector, because of the narrow price range, if costs increase they cannot be charged to the end user due to the nature of sales agreements.
- Creation of visual products is mainly based on detailed studies and this may decrease the efficiency and increase the costs.
- Because of the creativity based structure and high variety of products, difficulties may arise in using standard procedures and techniques.

A.1.4.2 Business Opportunities

- Easy to gain a competitive position, as potential entrepreneurs cannot enter into the market due to high cost barriers.
- Cultural richness in the region can be applied to product design and should be used as an opportunity to increase the market share.

A.1.5 Main Strategies

Within the existing market our products will always be perceived as creative and new. Product development will be our main strategy as shown in Table A.3.

Developing new product features:

- *Adapt*: Know-how will be brought through strategic alliances and will be adapted to the organization. As being a pioneer in the market, this will be an advantage for substantial product development.
- *Modify*: The technology and theme (characters, soundtracks, etc.) used will be updated according to the market requirements and changing preferences of customers.
- *Minify*: IPhone applications will be created for our trailers integrated with social media.
- *Substitute*: Our products will be applied to the toys of movies, such as animal characters, etc.
- *Combine*: Selling special designed (logos, themes, shapes) 3D eyeglasses to the movie audiences.

We will also focus on differentiation as a strategy shown in Table A.4, by using our differentiation as a competitive advantage on a narrow scale market.

Table A.3   Components of Strategy

		MARKET	
		NEW	EXISTING
PRODUCT	NEW	Innovation	Product development
	EXISTING	Market development	Market concentration

Table A.4   Generic Strategies

		COMPETITIVE ADVANTAGE	
		COST	DIFFERENTIATION
SCOPE	BROAD	Cost leadership	Differentiation
	NARROW	Cost focusing	Differentiation focusing

A.2 Y Technologies

Vision:

Make technology invisible for providing total satisfaction for our customers, and opportunities for our associates to grow and contribute.

Mission:

Y Technologies is targeting to enhance our customers' businesses by providing consultancy on software and hardware development for telecom companies in the field of information technology with its international experience to move to a superior position in the market.

We provide a full range of consultancy services and support to help removing the hassles out of your IT projects.

A.2.1 Internal Analysis

Strengths will include the following:

- Firm's products/services; breadth of product line
- Ability to gather needed information about markets
- Product/service mix and expansion potential
- Channels of distribution: number, coverage, and control
- Effective sales organization: knowledge of customer needs
- Product/service image, reputation, and quality
- Pricing strategy and pricing flexibility
- Procedures for digesting market feedback and developing new products, services
- After-sale service and follow-up
- Ability to raise short-term capital
- Ability to raise long-term capital: debt/equity
- Cost of capital relative to industry and competitors
- Relations with owners, investors and stockholders
- Leverage positions

- Cost of entry and barriers to entry
- Price-earnings ratio
- Effective cost control, ability to reduce costs
- Efficient and effective accounting system for cost, budget, and profit planning
- Economies of scale
- Effective use of subcontracting
- Degree of vertical integration, value added, and profit margin
- Efficiency and cost/benefit of equipment
- Effective operation control procedures
- Research and development/technology/innovation
- Patents, trademarks, and similar legal protection
- Management personnel
- Employees' skill and morale
- Efficient and effective personnel policies
- Effective use of incentives to motivate performance
- Ability to level peaks and valleys of employment
- Employee turnover and absenteeism
- Specialized skills
- Organizational structure
- Firm's record for achieving objectives
- Organization of communication system
- Overall organizational control system
- Organizational climate, culture
- Top-management skill, capacities, and interest
- Strategic planning system
- Intraorganizational synergy

Weaknesses will include the following:

- Concentration of sales in a few products or to a few customers
- Market share or submarket shares
- Imaginative, efficient and effective sales promotion and advertising
- Goodwill/brand loyalty
- Corporate-level resources
- Tax considerations
- Working capital; flexibility of capital structure

- Financial size
- Inventory control systems; inventory turnover
- Cost and technological competencies relative to industry and competitor's
- Labor relations cost compared to industry and competition
- Experience
- Firm's image and prestige
- Use of systematic procedures and techniques in decision making

A.2.2 Environmental Analysis

A.2.2.1 Macroeconomic Analysis   Macroeconomic analysis summarizes the status of the variables with respect to customers, government, financial institutions, suppliers, shareholders and employees point of views.

On the demographical side, population growth rate has a low impact on the IT business environment.

On the economic side, growth rate, interest rate, exchange rate, and inflation rate are the factors that have high impact on the IT business environment.

On the political side, government regulations and policies that have a huge impact on IT operations may include trade and labor laws, tax policies, environmental laws and regulations, trade restrictions, commercial tariffs, infrastructure and development policies. The degree of political stability also has an important impact on IT business environment.

On the technological side, R and D activities, automation, technology incentives, and rate of change have a high impact on IT operations.

On the social side, changes in social trends such as health consciousness, career attitudes, emphasis on safety and change in life styles have normal impact on the demand for IT services.

A.2.2.2 Competition Analysis   Figure A.4 shows the competition analysis worksheet that helps us to analyze shows the status of the existing firms, threats of new companies, competitive power of customers and suppliers.

	FIRMS IN THE INDUSTRY					THREATS OF NEW COMPANIES						COMPETITIVE POWER OF CUSTOMERS							COMPETITIVE POWER OF SUPPLIERS			
	Quantity of firms in the industry	Growth rate of the industry	Differences and the specialties of the products	Fixed costs	Cost to leave the industry	Costs of the companies in the industry related with the company size	Firms which have the customer-firm loyalty	The equity needed to enter the industry	Ability to reach channel of distribution	Cost advantage related with experience	Barriers to enter the industry	The share of the customer in the whole sale	Potential of production of the products by integration	Alternative suppliers	Cost of the change of the suppliers	Flexibility in the prices	The importance of the service for the customers	Quantity of firms in the industry	Providing unique products/services	Substitute goods in the market	Potential of production of the products by integration	The share of the sale of the supplier
High	0	1	1	0	0	0	0	0	0	1	0	1	1	0	0	0	0	1	1	1	0	0
Avg.	0	0	0	1	0	1	0	1	1	0	1	0	0	0	0	0	1	0	0	0	1	1
Low	1	0	0	0	1	0	1	0	0	0	0	0	0	1	1	1	0	0	0	0	0	0

Figure A.4 Competition analysis table.

A.2.2.3 Industry Life Cycle   Our industry is in growth stage shown in Figure A.5

A.2.3 Competitive Advantages, Success Factors, Weaknesses

Table A.5 is a comparison table that ends-up with competitive advantages, success factors and weaknesses of the firm. In short, we can say that:

- *Competitive advantages*: Factors providing the business with an edge compared to its main competitor and industry average, that is, the ones that have plus sign only on the Co. Y column.
- *Success factors*: Factors that are important capabilities for the business to have but are also typical of every viable competitor and do not represent a potential source of any strategic advantage.
- *Key vulnerabilities*: Factors on which the business currently lacks the necessary skill, knowledge, or resources to compete effectively, and shown as minus sign on the Co. Y column.

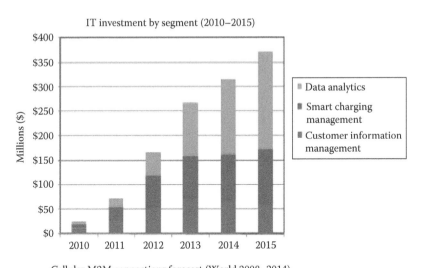

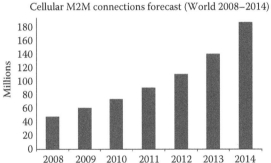

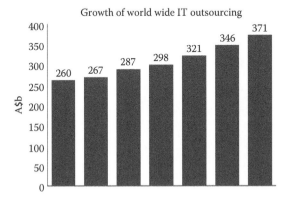

Figure A.5   Industry life cycle.

Table A.5   Comparison Table

		INDUSTRY	Y TEC.	MAIN RIVALRY
Marketing	Firm's products/services; breadth of product line	+	+	+
	Concentration of sales in a few products or to a few customers	−	−	−
	Ability to gather needed information about markets	−	+	+
	Market share or submarket shares	+	−	+
	Product/service mix and expansion potential	−	+	−
	Channels of distribution: number, coverage and control	+	+	+
	Effective sales organization: knowledge of customer needs	−	+	+
	Product/service image, reputation and quality	+	+	+
	Imaginative, efficient and effective sales promotion and advertising	−	−	−
	Pricing strategy and pricing flexibility	−	+	−
	Procedures for digesting market feedback and developing new products, services	+	+	+
	After-sale service and follow-up	+	+	−
	Goodwill/brand loyalty	−	−	−
Finance and Accounting	Ability to raise short-term capital	−	+	+
	Ability to raise long-term capital: debt/equity	−	+	+
	Corporate-level resources	−	−	−
	Cost of capital relative to industry and competitors	+	+	+
	Tax considerations	−	−	−
	Relations with owners, investors, and stockholders	+	+	+
	Leverage positions	+	+	+
	Cost of entry and barriers to entry	+	+	−
	Price-earnings ratio	−	+	+
	Working capital; flexibility of capital structure	−	−	+
	Effective cost control, ability to reduce costs	−	+	−
	Financial size	+	−	+
	Efficient and effective accounting system for cost, budget, and profit planning	−	+	+

(Continued)

Table A.5 (*Continued*)   Comparison Table

		INDUSTRY	Y TEC.	MAIN RIVALRY
Production/ Technical	Inventory control systems; inventory turnover	−	−	−
	Economies of scale	−	+	+
	Effective use of subcontracting	−	+	+
	Degree of vertical integration, value-added and profit margin	+	+	+
	Efficiency and cost/benefit of equipment	+	+	+
	Effective operation control procedures	+	+	+
	Cost and technological competencies relative to industry and competitors	−	−	−
	Research and development/ technology/innovation	−	+	−
	Patents, trademarks and similar legal protection	−	+	+
Personnel	Management personnel	−	+	+
	Employees' skill and morale	+	+	−
	Labor relations cost compared to industry and competition	−	−	−
	Efficient and effective personnel policies	+	+	+
	Effective use of incentives to motivate performance	+	+	+
	Ability to level peaks and valleys of employment	−	−	+
	Employee turnover and absenteeism	+	+	+
	Specialized skills	+	+	+
	Experience	+	−	+
Organization and General Management	Organizational structure	+	+	+
	Firm's image and prestige	−	−	+
	Firm's record for achieving objectives	+	+	+
	Organization of communication system	+	+	+
	Overall organizational control system	−	+	+
	Organizational climate, culture	+	+	+
	Use of systematic procedures and techniques in decision making	−	−	−
	Top-management skill, capacities, and interest	−	+	+
	Strategic planning system	+	+	+
	Intraorganizational synergy	+	+	+

A.2.3.1 Competitive Advantages Competitive advantages are as follows:

- Product/service mix and expansion potential
- Pricing strategy and pricing flexibility
- After-sale service and follow-up
- Effective cost control
- Research and development/technology/innovation.

A.2.3.2 Success Factors

- Firm's products /services; breadth of product line
- Ability to gather needed information about markets
- Relations with owners, investors, and stockholders
- Efficient and effective accounting system for cost, budget, and profit planning
- Degree of vertical integration, value–added, and profit margin
- Effective use of subcontracting
- Patents, trademarks, and similar legal protection
- Specialized skills
- Organizational structure
- Firm's image and prestige
- Firm's record for achieving objectives
- Overall organizational control system.

A.2.3.3 Weaknesses

- Market share or submarket shares
- Working capital; flexibility of capital structure
- Cost and technological competencies relative to industry and competitors
- Firm's image and prestige
- Use of systematic procedures and techniques in decision making
- Ability to level peaks and valleys of employment
- Concentration of sales in a few products or to a few customers
- Imaginative, efficient and effective sales promotion and advertising
- Goodwill/brand loyalty

- Corporate-level resources
- Experience
- Tax considerations
- Inventory control systems; inventory turnover
- Cost and technological competencies relative to industry and competitors
- Labor relations cost compared to industry and competition
- Use of systematic procedures and techniques in decision making.

A.2.4 Scenarios and Opportunities

A.2.4.1 Positive and Negative Scenarios   The concluded positive and negative scenarios are shown in Figures A.6 and A.7.

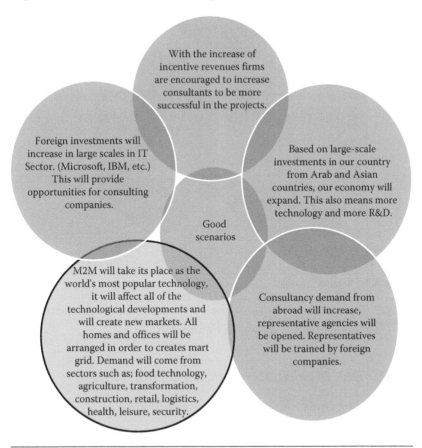

Figure A.6   Positive scenarios.

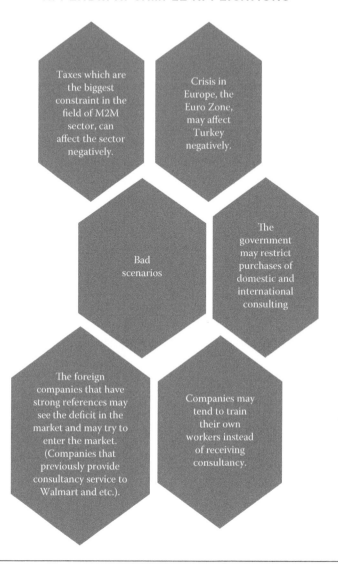

Figure A.7   Negative scenarios.

A.2.4.2 Business Opportunities   The concluded business opportunities for Y Technologies are shown in Figure A.8.

A.2.5 Strategic Objectives, Main Goals, and Grand Strategies

A.2.5.1 Main Goals   Financial goals are as follows:

- Exceed $5 million in the next 10 years
- Increase revenue by 15% annually

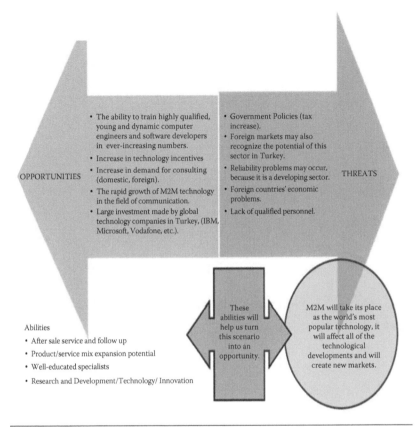

Figure A.8 Business opportunities for Y Technologies.

- Increase gross profit by 15% annually
- Increase contracts with companies by 10% annually.

Operational goals are as follows:

- Continuously improve operational processes
- Capitalize on physical facilities (location, capacity, etc.)
- Improve organizational structure
- Restructure available resources
- Decrease expenses by 5%
- Improve overall productivity.

A.2.5.2 Main Strategies Product development will be the main strategy that is shown in Figure A.9. This involves investing heavily in research and development for developing new technologies for telecom companies.

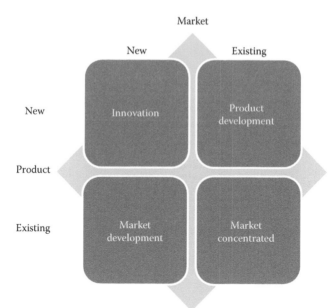

Figure A.9 Components of strategy.

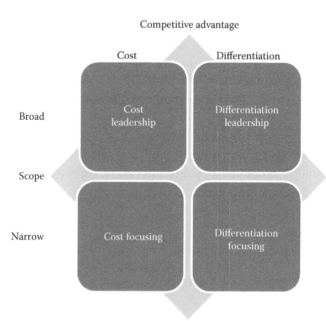

Figure A.10 Generic strategies.

Y Technologies aims to utilize its differentiation advantage for a few selected number of segments in which existing competitors could not meet their requirements. Table A.10 shows the selected strategy. Y Technologies will offer specially tailored software and hardware consultancy to its customers for a premium price.

Appendix B: Brainstorming

Brainstorming, with the extensive definition, is a form of meeting arranged to produce creative ideas. The ideas produced are intended to reach a solution, to support the decision-making process, to compose scenarios, and/or to find out competitive advantages.

brainstorming is a commonly used participative and practical technique in order to let the organizations develop strategies to reach an efficient and profitable structure.

The intention of brainstorming is to create a radical thinking environment, to adopt a simple and mutual systematic thinking, to examine agreements and assumptions, and to reach a solution by consensus.

B.1 Preparatory Works

- In order to manage brainstorming, it will be beneficial
    - To reach a required solution by brainstorming, in other words to reveal the intention of brainstorming
    - To determine the sources of the results required to be reached
    - To well understand and define the problems to be solved
    - To determine the developments and trends on the issues to be addressed
- The trends, opinions, and ideas to be evaluated can cover the following aspects of the issue:
    - History
    - Current condition
    - Future
    - Significant and global trends
    - Main trends and generally agreed concepts
    - Issues beyond normal that arise interest
- It is beneficial to perform a status analysis regarding the issue before starting brainstorming.

B.2 Premeeting

If possible, locations except office should be selected for the meeting. Location selected for brainstorming should be indoors and isolated as much as possible.

It would be beneficial to inform the individuals who will participate in the meeting beforehand regarding the issue and to give a specific period—such as 1 week—to think, practice, and generate ideas on the issue.

As this approach will enable the participants to generate more ideas during brainstorming, it can also cause the participants to effect each other by discussing before brainstorming, and hence, informing the participants beforehand shall be left as the decision of the meeting manager.

B.3 Brainstorming Meeting

Brainstorming meetings should be held in a disciplined environment but away from formality. Number of individuals attending the brainstorming meetings should not be excessive and it should be limited according to the intention of brainstorming, meeting hall, and time to be allocated for the meeting. The participants of equal levels of knowledge and experience will be beneficial for everyone to make their point.

Brainstorming meetings should be active, alive, and loud as much as possible. It will be beneficial to have the brainstorming meetings managed by a meeting manager.

It is not necessary that the attendants who participated in brainstorming meeting have experience in the subject area. This condition will make the brainstorming meetings beneficial and reach right solution.

Recorder should not be used during the brainstorming, as the participants would not like it. Everyone should actively participate in the sessions.

B.4 Start of Meeting

Prior to brainstorming meeting, the meeting manager should clearly communicate with the participants about the intention of the meeting, the result required to be obtained, and the source of the result required to be obtained.

The meeting manager should enlighten the participants regarding the sections of the meeting and the length of each section. It will make the meeting more efficient. Being adhered to time is the duty of the meeting manager.

The meeting will be effective if the meeting manager should begin the meeting with the entertaining and interesting questions. Initially, written expression of the opinions is recommended in respect of accelerating the adaptation process of the participants.

B.5 Generating Ideas

All the participants should be provided with speaking rights in a disorderly manner. Here, everyone is allowed to share their opinions, and therefore, the approach is mostly recommended.

Everyone should speak in turns and express all kinds of their opinions regarding the issue without being interrupted. A specific idea is selected and other ideas that evoke the meetings are encouraged.

Parallel thinking is required from the participants, that is, thinking positively and then negatively by expressing their ideas.

As an extension of the parallel-thinking approach, the six-hat method of *Edward de Bono* can be used. During the application of this method, it is expected that the participants wear various hats and make interpretations over the perspectives given by these hats. These perspectives are as follows: being objective, being emotional, being a risk taker, being positive, being a creative freak, and being judgmental.

During brainstorming, meeting manager should provide an environment for all the participants to speak. Here, the point not to be ignored is that, the silence of the participants arises from their thinking requirements, being unable to leave their shyness at first, from their mistrust against the environment, etc. The meeting manager should specify the ideas by repetitions. Differences can arise on the second expression of an idea.

During the generation of ideas, the meeting manager shall not make any interpretations, shall not make criticisms and shall not involve in evaluations. The meeting manager should accept the ideas with maturity. An idea seeming to be superficial can assist on the rise of an idea that will lead to a real result.

Providing not to diverge from the issue during the generation of ideas or assembling the diverged issue is the duty of the meeting manager. Meeting manager can ask questions, such as *how, where, when, why,* in order to accelerate the meeting.

Meeting manager should remind the intention of the meeting during brainstorming. When the definition of intention by the first brainstorming is not able to assist on generation of ideas, a second definition shall be selected.

A work session that turned to be inefficient shall not be pushed to continue. It is beneficial to conclude the brainstorming sessions with the most unimagined ideas. This will assist the rise of different ideas.

During brainstorming, all ideas should be numbered and written on a *flip chart* by the meeting manager. The writing shall be with a pen that is nonerasable and that attracts everyone's attention. All ideas shall be placed on the wall side to side as to provide everyone to see. During writing, it is important not to spoil the fluency of brainstorming and to use abbreviations in order to provide the rise of new ideas.

B.6 Evaluation of Ideas

Elimination is applied on all the assembled ideas. To facilitate the elimination, the assembled list should be allocated to subgroups (economic, social, technological, and legal). It will be beneficial to perform the elimination of the participants.

During the elimination, the meeting manager can use various techniques. For example, the ideas being really critical and being impossible to be estimated and that cannot be controlled to be kept and the others can be removed from the list according to the requirements of the meeting manager.

B.7 Developing Scenarios

Participants should be grouped by the meeting manager in different rooms in order to develop scenario drafts. Each group had the eliminated list of the scenario.

Scenarios are developed by the groups on the progress of the addressed issue by following the list if a list is given, or by requiring the groups to keep the ideas in their memory if a list is not given.

The scenarios developed shall be consolidated by the relevant teams during the breaks and a common direction shall be obtained from the scenarios. At the last point, a common scenario should be formed.

Appendix C: Sample Outline for Strategic Plan and Functional Plans

A good strategic plan is between 25 and 50 pages long and takes at least 6 months to write.

Cover Letter

Only one thing is certain when you go hunting for money to start a business: you would not be the only hunter out there. It is necessary to make potential funders who wish to read your business plan instead of the hundreds of others on their desks. The cover letter should summarize the most attractive points of the project in few words as possible. It should be addressed to the potential investor by name.

Vision
Mission
Basic Policies
Executive Summary

This section should summarize the most important subjects of strategic plan and interconnect various sections.

It should be begin with a two-page or three-page management summary of the venture. It includes a short description of the business and discuss major goals and objectives.

It contains descriptions of company operations to date, potential legal considerations, and areas of risk and opportunity. The firm's financial condition was summarized and also past and current balance sheets, income and cash-flow statements, and other relevant financial records were included.

Strategic Plan

1. Status Analysis

   The status analysis section is expected but not to exceed three pages.

   Environmental Analysis

   This should consider external factors such as demographical, economical, legal, political, technological, and social changes, market dynamics, customer expectations, competitive conditions, strategies and objectives of competitors, suppliers, substitutes.

   - Macroeconomic analysis (global, national)
     - Demographical variables
     - Judicial–political variables
     - Economic variables
     - Sociocultural variables
     - Technological variables
   - Competition analysis
     - Rivalry
     - Suppliers
     - Customers
     - Substitutes
     - New arrivals
   - Industry life cycle

   Internal Analysis—Business Strengths and Weaknesses

   The phases of evolution experienced by the business from the past till today and the strengths and weaknesses caused by them on your business structure must be mentioned. This should consider internal factors such as labor force, technology, organization and management, operational matters, products and their market positions, financial characteristics, etc.

2. Competitive Advantages, Success Factors, and Weaknesses
3. Scenarios and Opportunities

Positive and Negative Scenarios for Industry
The potential positive and negative scenarios for your industry for the next 5 years must be mentioned, taking into consideration the major developments in your respective industry worldwide and in nation.
Business Opportunities and Threats
4. Strategic Objectives, Main Goals, Grand Strategies
The goals intended to be achieved during the next 5 years must be mentioned for each year, taking into consideration the following headings:
Strategic Objectives
Main Goals
- Financial and marketing goals
  - Which countries to be in
  - Regional concentration
  - Planned strategic partnerships
  - Alliances, merging, and acquisitions
  - Market goals
  - Financial goals
- Operational goals
  - Technological improvements
  - Organization
Grand Strategies
Business Risks
The key risks anticipated for the term of strategic plan must be reviewed in this section. Quantitative and qualitative risks must be indicated.

For example, a sensitivity analysis must be conducted, taking into consideration the probability that basic assumptions and parameters do not come about as expected, and the measures considered to be taken in this regard must be indicated.

Functional Plans

1. Marketing Plan
The competition should not be underestimated. Industry size, trends, and the target market segment were reviewed. Strengths and weaknesses of the product were discussed.

The most important things investors want to know are what makes the product more desirable than what's already available. Pricing to the competition should be compared. Sales must be forecasted in dollars and units. Outline sales, advertising, promotion, and public relation programs. The costs should agree with those projected in the financial statements, which are as follows:.

Market situation
Competitors and competition conditions
Target markets
Product
Price
Place
Promotion
Networking

2. Operational Plan

Minimum plant size, machinery required, production capacity, inventory and inventory-control methods, quality control, plant requirements, and so on are described. Estimates of product costs should be based on primary research.

Location and Facilities Analysis
The location of the business is one of the most important factors. A comprehensive demographic analysis of consumers, suppliers, etc., in the area of the proposed location is provided.

Technical Capability Analysis
Targeted Performances:
- Productivity
- Production quantities
- Scrap rate
- Return rate
- OEE

Required Investment Analysis and Feasibility Study
Proposed Personnel Requirements and Organization Structure
The organizational structure and phases anticipated for the next 5 years, as well as the associated HR needs and policy

must be indicated (roles and responsibilities considered to be added or modified, linkages among them, required skills and experience levels, major and summarized career plans, performance evaluation matters, wages and compensations, motivation program and policies, services considered to be outsourced)

3. Financial Plan

It is important to provide 5-year projections for income, expenses, and funding sources. one should be kept in mind that the business will not grow in a straight line. The planning should be adjusted to allow for funding at various stages of the business' growth. The rationale and assumptions used to determine the estimates must be explained. Assumptions should be reasonable and they are based on industry/historical trends. It is important to make sure that all totals add up and are consistent throughout the plan. The aforementioned points should be prepared by financial analyst.

The business person should be clear about excessively ambitious sales projections rather offer best-case, expected, and worst-case scenarios. These 5-year projections not only reveal how sensitive the bottom lines to sales fluctuations but also serve as good management guides.

Financial Analysis

Key ratios (sales/profit ratio, net-operating capital, etc.) must be selected and the way how these ratios can be improved during the term of the business plan must be analyzed.

- Income—sales analysis
- Operational expenses
  - Personnel analysis
  - Production/operations analysis
- Investments
- Profit/loss table
- Profit/loss analysis
  - Cost of goods sold analysis
  - General management expenses
- Balance sheet

Capital Expenses
Cash Flow
Opportunity Costs
Profitability calculation methods such as net present value and internal rate of return should be used.

Business Risks
Finance
It is necessary to indicate the amount of capital needed to commence or continue operations and describe how these fund are to be used. Make sure that the totals are the same as the ones on the cash-flow statement. This area will receive a great deal of review from potential investors, so it must be clear and concise.

Appendix
Provide a bibliography of all the reference materials you consulted.

Appendix D: Working Forms

This Appendix contains copies of the forms that are used for SSP. They may be used when solving your next strategic-planning problem. You may reproduce the copies of these forms for your own use, provided you recognize their original source, and hold their use within the copyright restrictions covering this book. Each of the forms included in this section is explained in the text and is listed in its order of appearance in the text.

FORM CODE	FORM TITLE
RICHARD MUTHER & ASS—756	Orientation Worksheet
IMECO—SSP—BH1	Business History Summary Table
IMECO—SSP—FA1	Internal Analysis-Functional Approach
IMECO—SSP—ME1	Macro-Economic Analysis Form
SSP—CA1	Competition Analysis Form
SSP—IF1	Evaluating Competitive Forces
SSP—FS1	Competitive Forces Status
IMECO—SSP—CC1	Comparison with Competitors & Ind.Avg.
IMECO—SSP—CW1	Competitive Advantages-Success Factors—Key Vulnerabilities
SSP—CI1	Certainty-Importance Grid
IMECO—SSP—DS1	Developing Alternative Scenarios
SSP—SA1	Market Attractiveness of a Scenario
SSP—BO1	Business Opportunities
IMECO—SSP—SO1	Selection of Opportunities—Prioritization

(Continued)

FORM CODE	FORM TITLE
IMECO—SSP—OG1	Strategic Objectives—Goals
SSP—CS1	Components of Strategy
SSP—GS1	Generic Competitive Strategies
RICHARD MUTHER & ASS—173	Factors Analysis Form
SSP—SO1	Strategic Option Grid
IMECO—SSP—AC1	Activity-Cost Table

Systematic Strategic Planning: A Comprehensive Framework for Implementation, Control, and Evaluation

Orientation Worksheet

Prepared by: _____ , Business: _____ .

Authorized by: _____ Project: _____ Date:_____ .

PROJECT ESSENTIALS

Objective(s) _____
External Condition(s) _____
Situation(s) _____
Scope/Extent _____

IMPORTANCE DESCRIPTION
A = Absolutely Important, O = Ordinary
E = Especially Important, U = Unimportant
I = Important Result, X = Beyond Control

PLANNING ISSUES	Imp.	Resp.	Proposed Resolution	Ok'd by
1.				
2.				
3.				
4.				
5.				
6.				

Dominance/Importance Rating   Mark "X" if beyond control

PLANNING SCHEDULE						Further Action
Task or Action Required to Plan	**Who**					
1.						
2.						
3.						
4.						
5.						
6.						
7.						
8.						
9.						

Reference Notes:_____

RICHARD MUTHER & ASSOCIATES – 756

Systematic Strategic Planning: A Comprehensive Framework for Implementation, Control, and Evaluation

Business History Summary Table

Prepared by: _____Business: _____

Authorized by: _____Project: _____ Date:_____

	Year	Year	Year	Year	Year	Year
PERSONNEL						
TECHNICAL						
ORGANIZATION and GENERAL MANAGEMENT						
PRODUCTION / OPERATIONS						
MARKETING						
FINACE and ACCOUNTING (x1000)						

IMECO - SSP – BH1

Systematic Strategic Planning: A Comprehensive Framework for Implementation, Control, and Evaluation

Functional Approach

Prepared by: _____ , Business: _____

Authorized by: _____ Project: _____ Date:_____

	FACTORS	Strengths/Weaknesses
MARKETING	Firm's products /services; breadth of product line	
	Concentration of sales in a few products or to a few customers	
	Ability to gather needed information about markets	
	Market share or submarket shares	
	Product / service mix and expansion potential	
	Channels of distribution: number, coverage and control	
	Effective sales organization	
	Product / service image, reputation and quality	
	Imaginative, efficient and effective sales promotion and advertising	
	Pricing strategy and pricing flexibility	
	Procedures for digesting market feedback and developing new products, services or markets	
	After-sale service and follow up	
	Goodwill/brand loyalty	
FINANCE AND ACCOUNTING	Ability to raise short-term capital	
	Ability to raise long-term capital: debt/equity	
	Corporate-level resources	
	Cost of capital relative to industry and competitors	
	Tax considerations	
	Relations with owners, investors and stockholders	
	Leverage positions	
	Cost of entry and barriers to entry	
	Price-earnings ratio	
	Working capital; flexibility of capital structure	
	Effective cost control, ability to reduce costs	
	Financial size	
	Efficient and effective accounting system for cost, budget and profit planning	
PRODUCTION/ OPERATIONS/ TECHNICAL	Raw materials cost and availability	
	Inventory control systems; inventory turnover	
	Location of facilities; layout and utilization of facilities	
	Economies of scale	
	Technical efficiency of facilities and utilization of capacity	
	Effective use of subcontracting	
	Degree of vertical integration, value added and profit margin	
	Efficiency and cost / benefit of equipment	
	Effective operation control procedures	
	Cost and technological competencies relative to industry and competitors	

Systematic Strategic Planning: A Comprehensive Framework for Implementation, Control, and Evaluation

		Research and development/technology/innovation	
		Patents, trademarks and similar legal protection	
PERSONNEL		Management personnel	
		Employees' skill and morale	
		Labor relations compared to industry and competition	
		Efficient and effective personnel policies	
		Effective use of incentives to motivate performance	
		Ability to level peaks and valleys of employment	
		Employee turnover and absenteeism	
		Specialized skills	
		Experience	
ORGANIZATION AND GENERAL MANAGEMENT		Organizational structure	
		Firm's image and prestige	
		Firm's record for achieving objectives	
		Organization of communication system	
		Overall organizational control system	
		Organizational climate, culture	
		Use of systematic procedures and techniques in decision making	
		Top-management skill, capacities and interest	
		Strategic planning system	
		Intraorganizational synergy	

IMECO - SSP – FA1

Systematic Strategic Planning: A Comprehensive Framework for Implementation, Control, and Evaluation

Macro-Economic Analysis Form

Prepared by: _____ , Business: _____ .

Authorized by: _____ ,Project: _____ Date:_____ .

	DEMOGRAPH				ECONOMICAL									JUDICIAL - POLITICAL					TECHNOLOGICAL					SOCIO - CULTURAL			
	Population growth	Age pattern	Immigration trends	Birth and death ratios	Education level	Change in GDP	Income distribution	Interest rates	Supply of cash	Inflation rate	Unemployment rate	Foreign exchange policy	Saving&consuming trends	Tax laws	Antitrust law	Incentives	Green laws	Business law	Political stability	R&D expenditures	Innovation opportunities	New products	Acceleration - tech. change	Fastness product supply	Increase in automation	Changes in life styles	Expectancy for career	Change in family structure	Changes in personal values
CUSTOMERS																													
GOVERNMENT																													
FINANCIAL INSTITUTIONS																													
SUPPLIERS																													
SHARE HOLDERS																													
EMPLOYEES																													
RESULT																													

+	Change for the better
	Same as before
-	Change for the worse

IMECO - SSP - ME1

Systematic Strategic Planning: A Comprehensive Framework for Implementation, Control, and Evaluation

Competition Analysis Form

Prepared by: _____ . Business: _____ .

Authorized by: _____ Project: _____ Date: _____

	FIRMS IN THE INDUSTRY					THREATS OF NEW COMPANIES						COMPETITIVE POWER OF CUSTOMERS						COMPETITIVE POWER OF SUPPLIERS					
	Quantity of firms in the industry	Growth rate of the industry	Differences and the specialties of the products	Fixed costs	Cost to leave the industry	Costs of the companies in the industry related with the company size	Firms which have the customer-firm loyalty	The equity needed to enter the industry	Ability to reach channel of distribution	Cost advantage related with experience	Barriers to enter the industry	The share of the customer in the whole sale	Potential of production of the products by integration	Alternative suppliers	Cost of the change of the suppliers	Flexibility in the prices	The importance of the product for the customers	Quantity of firms in the industry and the production place	Unique products sale	Substitute goods in the market	Potential of production of the products by integration	The share of the sale of the supplier
Low																						
Avg.																						
High																						

SSP – CA1

Systematic Strategic Planning: A Comprehensive Framework for Implementation, Control, and Evaluation

Evaluating Competitive Forces

Prepared by: _____ . Business: _____

Authorized by: _____ Project: _____ Date:_____

	FAVOURABLE	**NEUTRAL**	**UNFAVOURABLE**
VERY IMPORTANT	◯		
MODERATE		◯	
	◯		◯
UNIMPORTANT	◯		

SSP – IF1

Systematic Strategic Planning: A Comprehensive Framework for Implementation, Control, and Evaluation

Competitive Forces Status

Prepared by: _____ . Business: _____ .

Authorized by: _____ Project: _____ Date:_____ .

ENTRANTS

SUPPLIER   RIVALRY   BUYER

SUBST.

✓✓ Very favorable
✓ Neutral

SSP – FS1

Systematic Strategic Planning: A Comprehensive Framework for Implementation, Control, and Evaluation

Comparison with Main Competitors and Industry Average

Prepared by: _____ . Business: _____ .

Authorized by: _____ Project: _____ Date: _____ .

	FACTORS	OUR BUSINESS	MAIN COMPETITOR(S)	INDUSTRY
MARKETING	Firm's products /services; breadth of product line			
	Concentration of sales in a few products or to a few customers			
	Ability to gather needed information about markets			
	Market share or submarket shares			
	Product / service mix and expansion potential			
	Channels of distribution: number, coverage and control			
	Effective sales organization			
	Product / service image, reputation and quality			
	Imaginative, efficient and effective sales promotion and advertising			
	Pricing strategy and pricing flexibility			
	Procedures for digesting market feedback and developing new products, services or markets			
	After-sale service and follow up			
	Goodwill/brand loyalty			
FINANCE AND ACCUONTING	Ability to raise short-term capital			
	Ability to raise long-term capital: debt/equity			
	Corporate-level resources			
	Cost of capital relative to industry and competitors			
	Tax considerations			
	Relations with owners, investors and stockholders			
	Leverage positions			
	Cost of entry and barriers to entry			
	Price-earnings ratio			
	Working capital; flexibility of capital structure			
	Effective cost control, ability to reduce costs			
	Financial size			
	Efficient and effective accounting system for cost, budget and profit planning			

	Systematic Strategic Planning: A Comprehensive Framework for Implementation, Control, and Evaluation			
PRODUCTION/TECHNICAL	Raw materials cost and availability			
	Inventory control systems; inventory turnover			
	Location of facilities; layout and utilization			
	Economies of scale			
	Technical efficiency of facilities and utilization of capacity			
	Effective use of subcontracting			
	Degree of vertical integration, value added and profit margin			
	Efficiency and cost / benefit of equipment			
	Effective operation control procedures			
	Cost and technological competencies relative to industry and competitors			
	Research and development/technology/innovation			
	Patents, trademarks and similar			
PERSONNEL	Management personnel			
	Employees' skill and morale			
	Labor relations compared to industry and competition			
	Efficient and effective personnel policies			
	Effective use of incentives to motivate performance			
	Ability to level peaks and valleys of employment			
	Employee turnover and absenteeism			
	Specialized skills			
	Experience			
ORGANIZATION OF GENERAL MANAGEMENT	Organizational structure			
	Firm's image and prestige			
	Firm's record for achieving objectives			
	Organization of communication system			
	Overall organizational control system			
	Organizational climate, culture			
	Use of systematic procedures and techniques			
	Top-management skill, capacities and interest			
	Strategic planning system			
	Intraorganizational synergy			

IMECO - SSP – CC1

Systematic Strategic Planning: A Comprehensive Framework for Implementation, Control, and Evaluation

Competitive Advantages – Success Factors – Key Vulnerabilities

Prepared by: _____ , Business: _____ .

Authorized by: _____ Project: _____ Date: _____ .

	FACTORS	COMP. ADVANTAGES	SUCCESS FACTORS	KEY WEAKNESSES
MARKETING	Firm's products /services; breadth of product line			
	Concentration of sales in a few products or to a few customers			
	Ability to gather needed information about markets			
	Market share or submarket shares			
	Product / service mix and expansion potential			
	Channels of distribution: number, coverage and control			
	Effective sales organization			
	Product / service image, reputation and quality			
	Imaginative, efficient and effective sales promotion and advertising			
	Pricing strategy and pricing flexibility			
	Procedures for digesting market feedback and developing new products, services or markets			
	After-sale service and follow up			
	Goodwill/brand loyalty			
FINANCE AND ACCUONTING	Ability to raise short-term capital			
	Ability to raise long-term capital: debt/equity			
	Corporate-level resources			
	Cost of capital relative to industry and competitors			
	Tax considerations			
	Relations with owners, investors and stockholders			
	Leverage positions			
	Cost of entry and barriers to entry			
	Price-earnings ratio			
	Working capital; flexibility of capital structure			
	Effective cost control, ability to reduce costs			
	Financial size			
	Efficient and effective accounting system for cost, budget and profit planning			

	Systematic Strategic Planning: A Comprehensive Framework for Implementation, Control, and Evaluation			
PRODUCTION/TECHNICAL	Raw materials cost and availability			
	Inventory control systems; inventory turnover			
	Location of facilities; layout and utilization			
	Economies of scale			
	Technical efficiency of facilities and utilization of capacity			
	Effective use of subcontracting			
	Degree of vertical integration, value added and profit margin			
	Efficiency and cost / benefit of equipment			
	Effective operation control procedures			
	Cost and technological competencies relative to industry and competitors			
	Research and development/technology/innovation			
	Patents, trademarks and similar			
PERSONNEL	Management personnel			
	Employees' skill and morale			
	Labor relations compared to industry and competition			
	Efficient and effective personnel policies			
	Effective use of incentives to motivate performance			
	Ability to level peaks and valleys of employment			
	Employee turnover and absenteeism			
	Specialized skills			
	Experience			
ORGANIZATION OF GENERAL MANAGEMENT	Organizational structure			
	Firm's image and prestige			
	Firm's record for achieving objectives			
	Organization of communication system			
	Overall organizational control system			
	Organizational climate, culture			
	Use of systematic procedures and techniques			
	Top-management skill, capacities and interest			
	Strategic planning system			
	Intraorganizational synergy			

IMECO - SSP – CW1

Systematic Strategic Planning: A Comprehensive Framework for Implementation, Control, and Evaluation

Certainty-Importance Grid

Prepared by: _____. Business: _____.

Authorized by: _____Project: _____ Date:_____

	VERY CERTAIN	**UNCERTAIN**
VERY IMPORTANT		
LOW IMPORTANCE		

SSP – CI1

| *Systematic Strategic Planning: A Comprehensive Framework for Implementation, Control, and Evaluation* |

Developing Alternative Scenarios

Prepared by: _____ . Business: _____ .

Authorized by: _____ Project: _____ Date:_____ .

POSSIBLE FUTURE UNCERTAINTIES	Degree of Importance (a)	Likelihood-Occurrence (b)	Resultant Score (a)*(b)	To Be Considered

RATING DESCRIPTION

A	Abnormal Impact / Almost Certain to Occur (4)	O	Ordinary Impact / Only Small Likelihood (1)
E	Especially High Impact / Especially Likely to Occur (3)	U	Unimportant / Unlikely (0)
I	Important / Inclined to Occur (2)		

IMECO – SSP – DS1

Systematic Strategic Planning: A Comprehensive Framework for Implementation, Control, and Evaluation

Market Attractiveness of a Scenario

Prepared by: _____ . Business: _____ .

Authorized by: _____ Project: _____ Date:_____

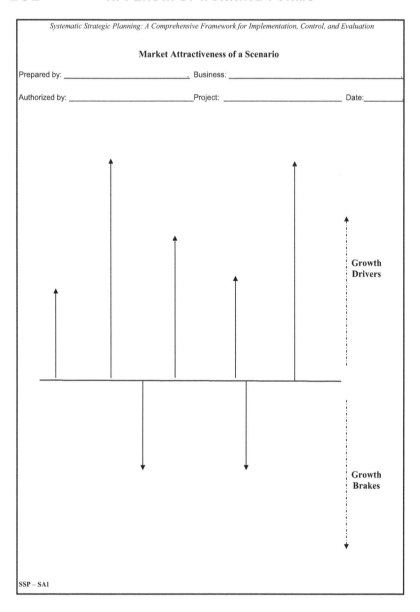

Growth Drivers

Growth Brakes

SSP – SA1

Systematic Strategic Planning: A Comprehensive Framework for Implementation, Control, and Evaluation

Business Opportunities

Prepared by: _____ . Business: _____

Authorized by: _____ Project: _____ Date: _____ .

SCENARIO MARKET ATTRACTIVENESS

	STRONG	MEDIUM	WEAK
HIGH	BIG BANG	Sunrise	Eclipse
MEDIUM	Milky Way	Neutral Zone	White Dwarf
LOW	Red Giant	Sunset	Blackhole

COMPETITIVE POSITION

SSP – BO1

Systematic Strategic Planning: A Comprehensive Framework for Implementation, Control, and Evaluation

Selection of Business Opportunities - Prioritization

Prepared by: _____ , Business: _____ .

Authorized by: _____ Project: _____ Date: _____ .

IMPLEMENTATION CAPABILITY	FINANCIAL ATTRACTIVENESS			
	Very High	High	Moderate	Low
A-Absolutely Capable				
E-Especially Capable				
I-Capable				
O-Very Little				
U-Uncertain				
X-Not Applicable				

The diameter of circle represents the relative position of an opportunity w.r.t. the market attractiveness and competitive position of it.

IMECO - SSP - SO1

Systematic Strategic Planning: A Comprehensive Framework for Implementation, Control, and Evaluation		

Strategic Objectives – Goals

Prepared by: _____ . Business: _____ .

Authorized by: _____ Project: _____ Date: _____

Opportunity

Strategic Objective

	GOAL	Description
FINANCIAL and MARKET	Target markets	
	Product range	
	Sales volume and profitability for the planned period	
	Comparative growth expectations	
	Countries to operate in	
	Regional concentration	
	Strategic partnerships considered	
OPERATIONAL/PERSONNEL/ MANAGEMENT	Organization	
	Training and experience	
	Wage and compensation	
	Investment goals	
	Labor turnover rate	

Systematic Strategic Planning: A Comprehensive Framework for Implementation, Control, and Evaluation

Safety regulations	
Environmental standards	
Technology and equipment choice	
Scrap rates	
Maintenance and repair policies	
Product standards	
Long-term capacity plans	
Production quantities	
Labor level	
Inventory level	
Overtime work	
Subcontractor	

IMECO - SSP - OG1

Systematic Strategic Planning: A Comprehensive Framework for Implementation, Control, and Evaluation

Components of Strategy

Prepared by: _____ Business: _____

Authorized by: _____ Project: _____ Date:_____

		MARKET	
		NEW	**EXISTING**
PRODUCT	**NEW**	DIVERSIFICATION	PRODUCT DEVELOPMENT
	EXISTING	MARKET DEVELOPMENT	MARKET PENETRATION

SSP – CS1

Systematic Strategic Planning: A Comprehensive Framework for Implementation, Control, and Evaluation

Generic Competitive Strategies

Prepared by: _____ Business: _____ .

Authorized by: _____ Project: _____ Date: _____ .

	COMPETITIVE ADVANTAGE	
	COST	**DIFFERENTIATION**
BROAD	COST LEADERSHIP	DIFFERENTIATION
NARROW	COST FOCUSING	DIFFERENTIATION FOCUSING

(SCOPE label on left axis spanning BROAD and NARROW)

SSP – GS1

Systematic Strategic Planning: A Comprehensive Framework for Implementation, Control, and Evaluation

Factors Analysis Form

Business: _____

Project: _____ Date: _____

Weighted by: _____ Rated by: _____ Approved by: _____

EVALUATING DESCRIPTION
A = Almost Perfect, O = Ordinary Result
E = Especially Good, U = Unimportant
I = Important Result, X =Not Acceptable

X. _____

Y. _____

Z. _____

V. _____

FACTOR/CONSIDERATION	WT.	ALTERNATIVE				
		X	Y	Z	V	W
1.						
2.						
3.						
4.						
5.						
6.						
7.						
8.						
9.						
10.						
TOT. Weighted Rated Down Total						

NOTES:

a. _____   d. _____

b. _____   e. _____

c. _____   f. _____

RICHARD MUTHER & ASSOCIATES – 173

Systematic Strategic Planning: A Comprehensive Framework for Implementation, Control, and Evaluation

Strategic Option Grid

Prepared by: _____ , Business: _____ .

Authorized by: _____ Project: _____ Date:_____ .

OPTIONS / CRITERIA	OPTION 1	OPTION 2	OPTION 3	OPTION 4
STRATEGIC ATTRACTIVENESS				
FINANCIAL ATTRACTIVENESS*				
IMPLEMANTATION DIFFICULTY				
UNCERTAINTY AND RISK				
ACCEPTABILITY (TO STAKE HOLDERS)				

Each criteria needs to be rated in terms of its attractiveness to the alternative as;

- ☒ high,
- ☒ medium,
- ☒ or low.

You need to reverse the ratings of uncertainty and difficulty.

SSP – SO1

Systematic Strategic Planning: A Comprehensive Framework for Implementation, Control, and Evaluation

Activity-Cost Table

Prepared by: _____ . Business: _____

Authorized by: _____ Project: _____ Date: _____

Strategic Objective 1

Goal 1.1

Activities	Current Year (t)	Budget Year (t+1)	Following First Year (t+2)	Following Second Year (t+3)
Activity 1.1.1				
Activity 1.1.2				
Activity 1.1.3				
Activity 1.1.4				
......				

IMECO - SSP – AC1

References

Aaker, D. A., Kumar, V., and G. S. Day. 2000. *Marketing Research*. Upper Saddle River, NJ: John Wiley & Sons.

Andrews, K. R. 1986. *The Concept of Corporate Strategy*. Columbus, OH: McGraw-Hill.

Ansoff, H. I. 1970. *Corporate Strategy*. London, U.K.: Penguin.

Avinash, K. D. and B. J. Nalebuff. 1993. *Thinking Strategically, the Competitive Edge in Business, Politics and Everyday Life*. New York: W. W. Norton & Company, Inc.

Bütüner, H. 2004. *Stratejik yönetim: Neden, nasıl?* Istanbul, Turkey: Rota Publications.

Clayton, S. 1995. *Sharpen Your Team Skills in Developing Strategy*. Columbus, OH: McGraw-Hill.

Ebert, R. J. and R. W. Griffin. 2000. *Business Essentials*. Upper Saddle River, NJ: Prentice Hall.

Fligor, M. 1990. *Brainstorming: The Book of Topics*. Storrs, CT: Creative Learning Press.

Harrison, J. S. and C. H. St. John. 2001. *Foundations in Strategic Management*. Evansville, IN: South-Western Publications.

Hax, A. C. and N. S. Majluf. 1996. *The Strategy Concept and Process: A Pragmatic Approach*. Upper Saddle River, NJ: Prentice Hall.

Hitt, M. A., Ireland, R. D., and R. E. Hoskisson. 2005. *Strategic Management: Competitiveness and Globalization*. Mason, OH: South-Western Thomson.

Hunger, J. D. and T. L. Wheelen. 2000. *Essentials of Strategic Management*. Upper Saddle River, NJ: Prentice Hall.

Keown, A. J. and J. Martin. 2001. *Financial Management: Principles and Applications*. Upper Saddle River, NJ: Prentice Hall.

213

Kotler, P. 2002. *Marketing Management: Analysis, Planning, Implementation &* *Control*. Englewood Cliffs, NJ: Prentice Hall.

Medura, J. 1998. *Introduction to Business*. Evansville, IN: South Western Publications.

Montgomery, C. A. and M. E. Porter. 1991. *Strategy: Seeking and Securing Competitive Advantage*. Watertown, MA: Harvard Business School Press.

Muther, R. 2006. *Reaching: Love Affairs with Industry*. Overland Park, KS: Leathers Publishing.

Muther, R. 2011. *Planning by Design*. Kansas City, MO: Institute for High Performance Planners.

Nickels, W. G., McHugh, J. M., and S. M. McHugh. 2002. *Understanding Business*. Columbus, OH: McGraw-Hill Higher Education.

Pearce, J. and R. Robinson. 2011. *Strategic Management: Formulation, Implementation and Control*. Columbus, OH: McGraw-Hill Higher Education.

Pietersen, W. 2002. *Reinventing Strategy: Using Strategic Learning to Create and Sustain Breakthrough Performance*. Hoboken, NJ: John Wiley & Sons.

Porter, M. E. 1980. *Competitive Strategy*. New York: The Free Press.

Porter, M. E. 1998. *Competitive Strategy: Techniques for Analyzing Industries and Competitors*. Florence, Italy: The Free Press.

Porter, M. E. 2002. *What Is Strategy?* HBR on Point Enhanced Edition. Watertown, MA: Harvard Business School Press.

Rasiel, E. M. 1999. *The McKinsey Way*. Columbus, OH: McGraw-Hill Trade.

Vernon, R. 1979. The product cycle hypothesis in a new international environment. *Oxford Bulletin of Economics and Statistics* 41(4): 255–267.

Wheelen, T. L. and J. D. Hunger. 2001. *Strategic Management and Business Policy*. Upper Saddle River, NJ: Prentice Hall.

Wickham, P. A. 2004. *Strategic Entrepreneurship*. London, U.K.: Pearson Education Limited.

Index